STATE V. BLOODWORTH

SECOND EDITION

STATE V. BLOODWORTH

SECOND EDITION

Joseph E. Taylor

Professor Emeritus, McGeorge School of Law
University of the Pacific

&

A.J. Griffith-Reed

Administration & Technology Specialist
Institute for Administrative Justice
McGeorge School of Law
University of the Pacific

NATIONAL INSTITUTE FOR TRIAL ADVOCACY

Address inquiries to:

Reprint Permission
National Institute for Trial Advocacy
1685 38th Street, Suite 200
Boulder, CO 80301-2735
Phone: (800) 225-6482
Fax: (720) 890-7069
Email: permissions@nita.org

ISBN 978-1-601-56-583-9
eISBN 978-1-601-56-584-6
FBA 1583

Printed in the United States of America

Official co-publisher of NITA.
WKLegaledu.com/NITA

CONTENTS

ACKNOWLEDGMENTS vii

DEDICATION. ix

INTRODUCTION. 1

SPECIAL INSTRUCTIONS FOR USE AS A FULL TRIAL 3

INFORMATION. 5

EXHIBITS

Exhibit 1—Transcript of 911 Call 9

Exhibit 2—Photo of Exhibit 2 on Table at Scene. 11

Exhibit 3—Photo Close-up of Exhibit 2 with Ruler Showing Size. 13

Exhibit 4—Photo of Kenneth Fletcher at Scene 15

Exhibit 5—Photo of Kenneth Fletcher Close-up at Scene 17

Exhibit 6—Photo of Pill Bottles at Scene 19

Exhibit 7—Diagram of Scene 21

Exhibit 8—CV of Dr. Tost 23

Exhibit 9—Photo of Fletcher's Yellow Corvette. 25

Exhibit 10—Facebook Page of Kenneth Fletcher. 27

Exhibit 11—Facebook Page of Billy Herman. 29

Exhibit 12—Facebook Page of Riverfront Plaza. 31

Exhibit 13—Facebook Page of Riverfront Plaza Party 33

Exhibit 14—Facebook Page of Gene Bloodworth 35

Exhibit 15—Facebook Page of Stag House Tavern. 37

Exhibit 16—Facebook page of Nita City Council 39

POLICE REPORTS

NCPD Burglary Offense Report by Detective Howard 43

NCPD Burglary Supplemental Report by Detective Howard 47

NCPD Murder Offense Report by Detective Howard. 53

NCPD Murder Offense Supplemental Report by Detective Howard. 57

NCPD Fingerprint Analysis Report. 59

Philadelphia Police Murder Offense Report. 61

MEDICAL REPORTS

Darrow County Medical Center Reports 69

Darrow County Medical Examiner's Report 77

Autopsy Report by Dr. Tost 79

      Body Diagram 83

      Head Diagram 85

Toxicology Report 87

ARREST RECORDS

Gene Bloodworth 91

Billy Herman 93

Sadie McLish 95

Chris Singleton 97

Kenneth Fletcher 99

PRELIMINARY HEARING TESTIMONY

Detective Lee Howard 103

Dr. Lou Tost 109

Billy Herman 113

Kerry Westlake 115

STATEMENTS OF DEFENSE WITNESSES

Chris Singleton 121

Sadie McLish 125

CORRESPONDENCE FROM DR. LESLIE SEWELL

Report of March 18, YR-1 131

Letter of January 15, YR-0 135

CV 137

APPENDICES

Applicable Nita Criminal Code and Vehicle Code Sections 141

Applicable Pennsylvania Criminal Code Section 145

Jury Instructions 147

Verdict Form 153

Acknowledgments

The authors would like to acknowledge the special contribution to the development of this case file made by Elizabeth Albers, MD, a forensic pathologist and medical consultant with the State of California Health Care Services Audits and Investigations and Medical Review Branch. She provided valuable expert advice on issues of toxicology and cause of death, and assisted greatly in the preparation of forensic pathology reports and testimony at preliminary hearing by the forensic pathologist in this case file. Without her assistance, the case file could not have been completed. The authors would also like to thank Sharon Cammisa for her contributions to the first edition, many of which still greatly influence the current version.

Professor Jay Leach of Pacific McGeorge School of Law perhaps made the greatest sacrifice of all when he agreed to play Kenneth Fletcher for the scene photo.

Thanks also to the 1947 Pittsburgh Pirates and Philadelphia Phillies baseball teams for providing the names of all characters in the *Bloodworth* case file.

The National Institute for Trial Advocacy wishes to thank Facebook for its permission to use likenesses of its website as part of these teaching materials.

DEDICATION

This publication is dedicated to the memory of Vincent W. Reagor, an outstanding lawyer who served first as an officer in the Reno Police Department, then as a Supervising Attorney and as Assistant Chief Deputy in the Sacramento County District Attorney's Office for nearly thirty years, and then served as a Senior Attorney and Special Prosecutor in the California Attorney General's Office for five years. Vince Reagor had a greater impact on the training of Deputy District Attorney Joseph Taylor than any other teacher or attorney. He taught me how to prepare cases for trial, how to present the case in court, and perhaps most important what ethical responsibilities prosecuting attorneys bear and how to fulfill those responsibilities. I worked with many prosecuting attorneys for over 22 years, and I place Vince Reagor at the top of that cast. Vince passed away this year, and I will dearly miss him.

Joseph E. Taylor

INTRODUCTION

State v. Bloodworth is a criminal case in which Gene Bloodworth, a former outfielder for the Pittsburg Pirates, has been charged with the first degree murder of Kenneth Fletcher, a realtor, in violation of § 101 of the Criminal Code of the State of Nita. On November 7, YR-2, Gene Bloodworth called the police to report that a man, who he believed was a resident of the condominium complex where he lived, came into his home at 1:30 a.m. armed with a knife. Bloodworth had punched him, and the man was lying unconscious on the floor. The 911 operator told him to kick the knife away in case Fletcher woke up.

When the police arrived, they wrote up a burglary and assault with a deadly weapon report and transported Fletcher to the hospital. Fletcher was examined and diagnosed with a subdural hematoma. At the hospital, Fletcher gave a statement to the police that he was at the condominium drinking with Bloodworth, and that Bloodworth had offered him a glass of whiskey and then struck him several times. He couldn't remember anything else until he woke up in the hospital with a terrible headache. Fletcher denied having a knife, and when shown the photo of the knife, Fletcher said he had never owned such a knife. Fletcher was treated and was released three days later on November 10, YR-2.

Three days later on November 13, YR-2, Fletcher was found unconscious outside his condominium. Responding fire department personnel determined he was dead. The Medical Examiner's Office was called and they transported Fletcher's body to the morgue. The State's forensic pathologist determined the cause of death was blunt force trauma to the head, and a significant medical finding was the presence of hepatic cirrhosis.

Further police investigation discovered another condominium resident, Billy Herman, who claimed to have overheard Bloodworth talking on his cell phone and heard him say that "if you mess with my stuff, I am going to mess with you."

The defendant has pled not guilty and contends that he was defending himself against a knife attack when Fletcher broke into his condo. He further contends that the injuries Fletcher received were not the cause of his death. A defense forensic pathologist has concluded that the autopsy findings are completely consistent with Bloodworth's version of the facts, and that Fletcher died from a combination of alcoholism and cirrhosis of the liver.

The applicable law is contained in the proposed jury instructions set forth at the end of the file.

SPECIAL INSTRUCTIONS FOR USE AS A FULL TRIAL

When this case file is used for a full trial, each party is limited to calling the following witnesses:

State of Nita: Billy Herman
                  Detective Lee Howard
                  Dr. Lou Tost
                  Kerry Westlake

Defendant: Gene Bloodworth
                  Dr. Leslie Sewell
                  Chris Singleton
                  Sadie McLish

DISCOVERY OBLIGATIONS

1) Pursuant to Nita C.C. § 1054.3, which requires the defense to disclose names, addresses, relevant written statements, and reports of witnesses the defense intends to call at trial, the reports of defense witnesses Chris Singleton, Sadie McLish, and Dr. Leslie Sewell have been disclosed to the prosecution.

2) Pursuant to Nita C.C. § 1054.2, Nita City Police Department case reports were disclosed to the defense by the prosecution.

REQUIRED STIPULATIONS

3) The defendant Gene Bloodworth is male. Sadie McLish is female. All other witnesses may be either male or female. Kenneth Fletcher was male.

4) The transcript of the 911 call marked Exhibit 1 is an accurate and complete transcript of the call made by the defendant to the Nita City Police Department at 2:15 a.m. on November 7, YR-2.

5) The fingerprint analysis report of Latent Fingerprint Examiner Joan Russell dated November 17, YR-2, is admissible as evidence. Counsel will stipulate to the qualifications of Ms. Russell to render an expert opinion as to the results of that examination.

PRE-TRIAL MOTIONS

6) The defendant moved to suppress all statement he made to Det. Howard on Fifth, Sixth, and Fourteenth Amendment grounds. The court ruled these statements were admissible.

7) The defendant moved to suppress any statements Kenneth Fletcher made to the police officers on the grounds that such statements are hearsay and on the ground that such statements are testimonial in violation of *Crawford v. Washington*, 541 U.S. 36 (2004). The defendant also moved to suppress all copies of Facebook pages collected by the Nita City Police Department, except the Nita City Council Facebook, page on grounds of lack of foundation and hearsay. The court reserved a ruling on both issues until the prosecution lays a foundation at trial.

OTHER INSTRUCTIONS

8) All years in these materials are stated in the following form:

    a)   YR-0 indicates the actual year in which the case is being tried (i.e., the present year);

    b)   YR-1 indicates the next preceding year (please use the actual year);

    c)   YR-2 indicates the second preceding year (please use the actual year), etc.

9) The legal issues that the court has ruled on may not be re-litigated at trial.

10) Electronic, color copies of exhibits can be found at the following website:

http://bit.ly/1P20Jea
Password: Bloodworth2

IN THE DISTRICT COURT OF THE STATE OF NITA
COUNTY OF DARROW

THE STATE OF NITA	)	
	)	Case No. CR 4219-YR-2
v.	)	
	)	INFORMATION
GENE A. BLOODWORTH	)	
Defendant.	)	
	)	

THE STATE OF NITA does hereby charge the defendant, GENE ANTHONY BLOODWORTH, with the following offense under the Criminal Code of the State of Nita:

That on 7th day of November, YR-2, at and within the County of Darrow and within the boundaries of Nita City, GENE A. BLOODWORTH committed the crime of murder in the first degree, a felony, in violation of Section 101 of the Criminal Code of the State of Nita, in that he did knowingly, willfully, feloniously, and deliberately, and with the intent to cause the death of Kenneth S. Fletcher, cause the death of Kenneth S. Fletcher, a human being, contrary to the form, force, and effect of the law of the State of Nita and against the peace and dignity of the People of the State of Nita.

DATED: July 24, YR-1

James Bagby
_____
Arthur Herring, Darrow County District Attorney
By James Bagby, Deputy District Attorney
County of Darrow, State of Nita

Exhibits

Exhibit 1

Transcript of 911 Call from Gene Bloodworth
November 7, YR-2, at 2:15 a.m.

The following is a verbatim transcript of the call received by Dispatcher Gables of the Nita City Police Department from Gene Bloodworth at 2:15 a.m. on November 7, YR-2.

Gables: 911, what's your emergency?

Bloodworth: Yes. I need to report a burglary. A man broke into my condo and was messing with my pills . . . trying to steal them, I guess. I hit him to get him out. As he was going down, I saw a glint in his hand. After he fell, I saw it was a knife.

Gables: Where at?

Bloodworth: He's in my condo. I had to hit him to stop him from using his knife. I think he's knocked out. I hit him pretty hard.

Gables: What's the address?

Bloodworth: It's Riverfront Plaza Condos. 4815 Riverfront Road, number 577 on the fifth floor. Can you hurry? I don't want him to wake up.

Gables: Okay, what's his name?

Bloodworth: Ah, I don't know him, but I think he goes by Butch. I don't know why he would try and rob me. He must be crazy.

Gables: Okay, where is the knife?

Bloodworth: Well, it's on the floor, right where he dropped it when I hit him.

Gables: Okay, I want you to go pick up the knife and put it in a safe place.

Bloodworth: Okay, okay. (Pause.)

Bloodworth: Okay, I put it away from him where he can't get it.

Gables: Okay. Officers will be at your home soon. I don't want you handling a knife. Do you understand? They might think you are dangerous. I don't want you near the knife when the officers arrive. Where did you put it? I don't want it to be near you when they arrive.

Bloodworth: I can put it on a night table on the other side of my condo and lead them there. Is that okay?

Gables: Right. Do that and don't touch anything else. When they arrive, tell them your name and let them in. Then you can point out the knife. If Butch begins to recover, leave your condo and go immediately to the first floor and see if you can contact someone in the condo office for your own safety. Do you understand?

Bloodworth: Yeah.

Gables: Okay. Is anybody else in the condo?

Bloodworth: No, just me.

Gables: Can you tell me, have you had problems before?

Bloodworth: Yeah.

Gables: Okay. What kind?

Bloodworth: Well, someone stole my wallet last week. Maybe it was him.

Gables: Okay. Officers are en route as we speak. They'll be there soon. Goodbye.

Bloodworth: Okay. Bye.

Exhibit 2

Photo of Exhibit 2 on Table at Scene

Exhibit 3

Photo Close-Up of Exhibit 2 with Ruler Showing Size

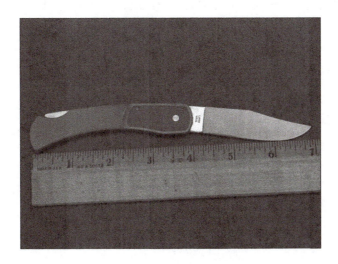

Exhibit 4

Photo of Kenneth Fletcher at Scene

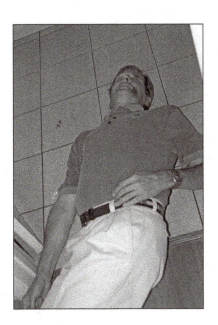

Exhibit 5

Photo of Kenneth Fletcher Close-up at Scene

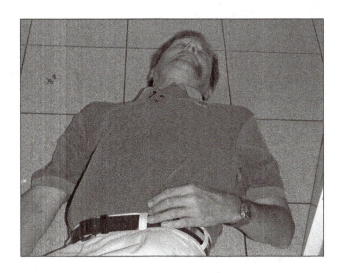

Exhibit 6

Photo of Pill Bottles at Scene

Exhibit 7

Diagram of Scene

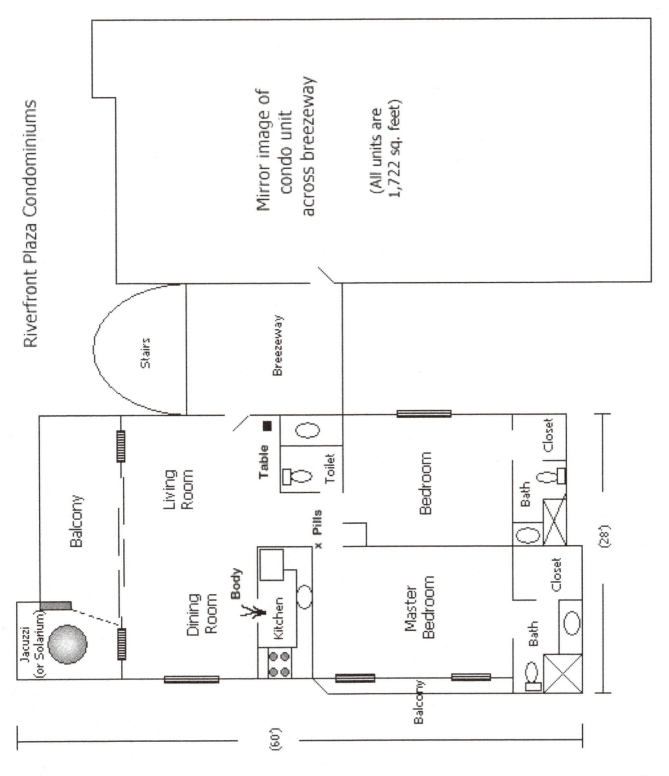

Exhibit 8

LOU TOST, MD
MEDICAL DIRECTOR, OFFICE OF THE DARROW COUNTY
MEDICAL EXAMINER'S OFFICE
1865 Government Drive, Suite 101
Nita City, Nita 85523-2102
(204) 555-1101

Education

YR-18 BS, Biology, Nita University
YR-16 MS Biology, Southern Methodist University
YR-13 MD, Case Western Reserve University
YR-10 Completed Residency in Anatomical and Clinical Pathology, Duke University Medical Center

Professional Experience

Assistant Chief Medical Examiner, Dr. Roscoe Phelps Fellowship, North Carolina University Medical Center, Chapel Hill, North Carolina YR-9
Forensic Pathologist, Diagnostic Pathology Medical Group, Nita City, Nita YR-8 to YR-6.
Assistant Director of Pathology, Darrow County Medical Examiner's Office, Nita City, Nita YR-6 to YR-5
Medical Director, Darrow County Medical Examiner's Office, Nita City, Nita YR-5 to present

Teaching Experience

Nita University Medical School, Adjunct Professor in Pathology, YR-5 to YR-2.
University of Southern Nita Medical School, Adjunct Professor in Pathology, YR-2 to present.

Professional Certifications and Associations

Physician's and Surgeon's License, North Carolina, YR-13
Physician's and Surgeon's License, Nita, YR-8
American Board of Pathology, Certification in Anatomic/Clinical Pathology, YR-7
American Board of Pathology, Certification in Forensic Pathology, YR-6
American Board of Forensic Examiners, YR-2
Member, Certification Board of the American Board of Pathology, YR-3 to present

Awards

Distinguished Member Award, Nita Association of Forensic Pathologists
Award of Merit, Nita Department of Justice

Professional Publications

Over 25 publications including journal articles entitled:
Autopsy Techniques in Blunt Force Trauma Cases, Standard Forensic Pathology, YR-5

Distinguishing Causes of Subdural Hematoma in Performing Autopsies, University of Nita Forensic Journal, YR-4

Necessity for Scientific Objectivity in Handling Legal Cases: *The Dilemma of Retention*, Law Enforcement Review, YR-2

Expert Testimony

In my work as a forensic pathologist, throughout my career I have performed approximately 2,000 medico-legal autopsies and assisted in or supervised other pathologists in approximately 100 other cases. I have testified in both state and federal courts of law and been found to be a qualified expert in forensic pathology in more than 110 cases.

Exhibit 9

Photo of Fletcher's Yellow Corvette

Exhibit 10

Facebook Page of Kenneth Fletcher

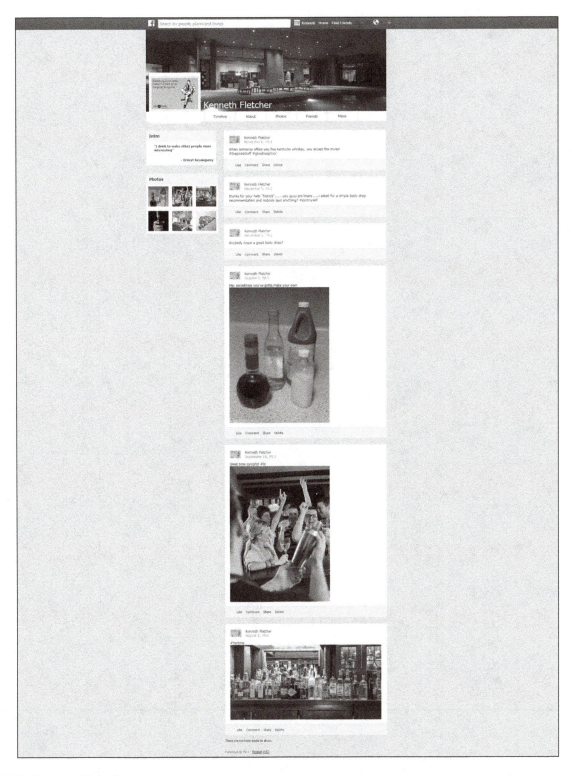

Exhibit 11

Facebook Page of Billy Herman

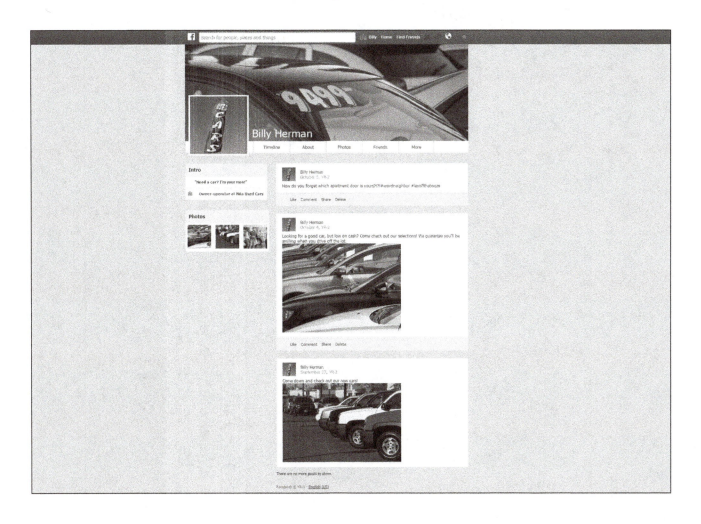

Exhibit 12

Facebook Page of Riverfront Plaza

Exhibit 13

Facebook Page of Riverfront Plaza Party

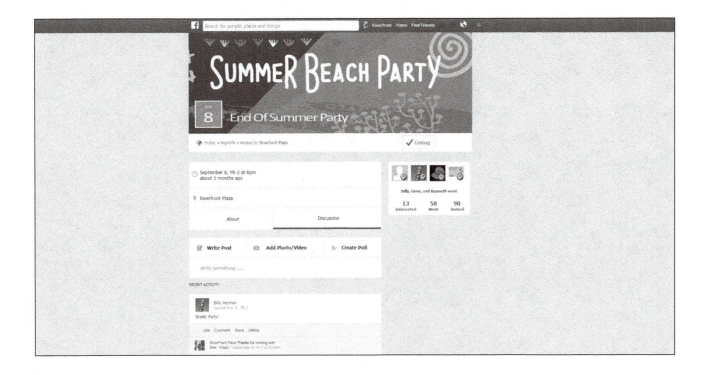

Exhibit 14

Facebook Page of Gene Bloodworth

Exhibit 15

Facebook Page of Stag House Tavern

Exhibit 16

Facebook Page of Nita City Council

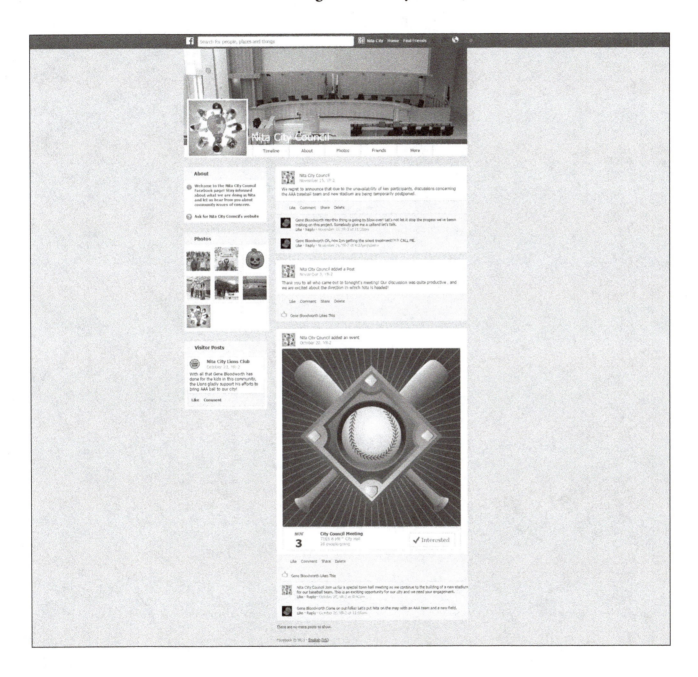

POLICE REPORTS

NITA CITY POLICE DEPARTMENT
OFFENSE REPORT

FILE NUMBER: YR-2-29088

VICTIM: Gene Anthony Bloodworth
4815 Riverfront Road #577
Nita City, Nita

SUSPECT: Kenneth S. Fletcher

LOCATION: 4815 Riverfront Road #577
Nita City, Nita

OFFENSE: CC 460—Burglary
CC 245—Assault with a Deadly Weapon
CC 211.c—Attempted Armed Robbery

DATE OF REPORT: November 7, YR-2

BY: Detective Lee Howard
Badge Number 214

DETAILS OF OFFENSE:

FACTS:

At 0215 hours, as the on-call detective of Crimes Against Persons, I was contacted by Lt. Mulcahy and directed to respond to the above address in a reported residential burglary in progress and felonious assault. The Riverfront Plaza is a high-end, rather elegant residential complex with expensive condos fronting on River Road and the Sterling River. I responded and arrived at the scene at 0230 hours. Officer Roe arrived moments later and helped secure the scene. I observed the suspect, later identified as Kenneth Fletcher, lying unconscious, the upper part of his body in the kitchen and his lower half in the dining area. I immediately took photos showing Fletcher's position. The suspect had some blood on his lips and forehead. There was a small amount of blood on the kitchen floor. There were several pill bottles on the floor in the doorway to the bedroom. While I was there, the suspect began to appear somewhat conscious and intoxicated, but he could not answer questions and was unable to stand up.

The victim, Gene Bloodworth, informed me that the suspect had gotten into the condo while he was sleeping and was going through his stuff. He said that he woke up and was afraid for his life. The man said something about "his money." Bloodworth jumped up and started punching him, trying to push him to the front door. He said he punched him really hard. As he punched he saw a "glint of light" in his hand. After he was down, Bloodworth realized it was a knife. Bloodworth said the knife fell from the suspect's hand to the floor, and Bloodworth immediately called 911. He said that the operator then told him to pick up the knife and place it in a safe place where the suspect could not get it. Bloodworth put the knife on a night table near the front door entrance. I photographed the knife in that position, and I then took custody of the knife and placed it carefully in a NCPD evidence envelope. I also checked the front door and there was no damage to the door or door frame or sign of forced entry. I asked Bloodworth if he had locked his door that night and he said, "Yeah. I think so."

Medic 20 of the Nita City Fire Department responded, and, due to the suspect not being able to answer basic questions, Elbie Greenberg of Medic 20 searched his billfold and identified him as Kenneth S. Fletcher. He was transported to the Darrow County Medical Center for treatment of his head injury. Because the suspect was going to be held for several days at the Medical Center, he was not immediately booked on the felony charges, as there was time to conduct further investigation. I then took a detailed statement from Bloodworth, which is outlined below, and I canvassed the condominium complex to determine if there were any other witnesses. Due to the late hour, I was unable to locate anyone in the complex who witnessed any of the activities that early morning.

STATEMENT OF GENE ANTHONY BLOODWORTH:

I don't know this man Fletcher, but he is familiar. I may have dealt with him before, you know, small talk a time or two in the past at the condo, but I really don't know him. I do remember that he drove a fancy car, I believe a Corvette, yellow in color, that was missing part of the front end. I was asleep and was awakened by a noise of some kind, sounded like a bumping noise. I first thought I had left my 3D TV set on in the living room. It was sometime around 2:00 in the morning. I saw a male standing in the doorway of my bedroom. I said, "What are you doing here?" He came toward me. I jumped out of bed and we started fighting. He was swinging at me but he missed. I hit him a couple of times and forced him into the dining area. He swung at me some more, and it looked like he was off balance while he was going backwards. In the dining area while he was swinging at me, I saw the light from the outside glare off something in his hand while he swung. I hit him a couple of more times. He was knocked out and lying on the floor. I called 911 and told them what happened. I then saw the knife in his hand. I told the lady on the phone he had a knife. She told me to get it away from him. I kicked the knife away from him. He was still lying on the floor between the dining area and the kitchen. I think he started to get up when he was coming around.

I didn't know there was a knife in his hand until I knocked him out. I was afraid because this guy was in my house and I didn't know what he was doing. I wanted to stop him before he could do anything else. The medications on the floor are mine and my girlfriend's. The guy must have taken them from the back of my room and dropped them and that woke me up. Like I said, I've seen this guy before in the complex, but I don't know who he is. I think he lives on another floor in the building. Two nights ago someone broke into my condo and stole my wallet. I think I locked the door, but I'm not positive. I am pretty sure I did. I don't know if he had a key to get in. He certainly did not have my permission to come into my condo. I want to press charges.

EVIDENCE BOOKED:

Item #1—Transcript of 911 call from Gene Bloodworth to NCPD.
Item #2—One digital photo of knife lying on table at scene.
Item #3—One digital photo of knife with ruler showing size of knife.
Item #4—One digital photo of Kenneth Fletcher lying between the dining area and the kitchen.

Item #5—One close-up digital photo of Kenneth Fletcher lying between dining area and kitchen areas.

Item #6—One digital photo of pill bottles lying on floor.

Item #7—One diagram of scene showing position of Kenneth Fletcher on floor, location of knife, and location pill bottles.

Item #8—One 7-inch knife recovered on the floor in the condominium of Gene Bloodworth and identified by Bloodworth as the knife that Fletcher used in his attack.

All of the above items were booked in NCPD Evidence Section for safekeeping.

FURTHER INVESTIGATION:

1) Contact neighbors in the complex to determine the suspect's motives and conduct and what relationship he had with the victim.

2) How was the suspect able to make entry?

3) Did suspect make any statement to medical personnel and was any of the victim's property on suspect's person when taken to the hospital?

4) Obtain statement from suspect.

5) Check to see if Fletcher had a Yellow Corvette.

FILE NUMBER: YR-2-29088

VICTIM: Gene Anthony Bloodworth
4815 Riverfront Road #577
Nita City, Nita

SUSPECT: Kenneth S. Fletcher

LOCATION: 4815 Riverfront Road #577
Nita City, Nita

OFFENSE: CC 460—Burglary
CC 245—Assault with a Deadly Weapon
CC 211.c—Attempted Armed Robbery

DATE OF REPORT: November 14, YR-2

BY: Detective Lee Howard
Badge Number 214

STATEMENT OF BILLY HERMAN:

On November 8, YR-2, at 1420 hours, I spoke with Herman, who stated that he lives at the Riverfront Plaza in Suite 408. Herman has resided at this condominium complex for over three years and knows both Fletcher and Bloodworth. On a number of occasions, Herman has seen Fletcher obviously under the influence of alcohol, and it is common knowledge that Fletcher had a drinking problem. So far as Herman knows, Fletcher has never been violent, but Herman understood that Fletcher had suffered financial difficulties lately, largely due to the slowdown in real estate sales and over-extension of Fletcher's business activities. As a result, in Herman's opinion Fletcher has been using more alcohol and possibly drugs recently.

Herman has seen Bloodworth and Fletcher together on at least two occasions. There was a Plaza out-door party on the lawn next to the river about two or three months ago, and Fletcher appeared drunk. The gathering was not only for residents of the Riverfront Plaza residents, but also for members of the Nita City Chamber of Commerce, and is held annually in early in September. Herman said the following:

> I couldn't hear exactly what they were saying, but Bloodworth appeared to be angry. I remember him saying something like, "Don't try that again with me." I have no idea what he meant. Fletcher just walked away and sat down on a lawn chair with his drink. About a month ago, both were on the elevator when I went to the fourth floor, and Fletcher got off when I did. Fletcher asked me if

I lived on the fourth floor, and I told him I did. Fletcher then said he didn't, but he didn't want to ride any further with Bloodworth. I don't know why.

Herman said that on one occasion Herman opened the front door of Herman's condo to leave and saw Fletcher holding on to the outside doorknob. This was about 9:30 in the evening, and Herman said, "What are you doing here?" Fletcher said something like, "I must have gotten the wrong condo, and I am very sorry for disturbing you," and he walked away. Fletcher seemed to be staggering a bit as he walked. Herman thought about reporting this to security, but decided not to, as Herman may have just been drunk.

Herman remembers about ten days ago that Bloodworth was standing near the Plaza office and talking on his cell phone. He heard Bloodworth say, "If you mess with my stuff, I'm going to mess with you." Herman didn't know who Bloodworth was talking to, but Herman later did wonder whether it was related to the incident in Bloodworth's condo.

Herman said that Fletcher never appeared to be violent or angry. If anything, Fletcher appeared at times to be sort of a sympathetic drunk who was down on his luck. Herman thought that was sad, as Fletcher Realtors was well known and successful for a number of years as he said, "until the market went south and his wife divorced him."

STATEMENT OF KERRY WESTLAKE:

On November 8, YR-2, at 1535 hours, I spoke with Westlake. Westlake is the manager of Riverside Plaza. Westlake was not informed of the burglary and assault until around 7:00 a.m. on the morning of November 7 when a resident told Westlake that the police had arrested a burglar on the fifth floor.

Westlake does know Bloodworth and has had several conversations about Bloodworth's previous career as a major league ball player for the Pirates. In fact, Westlake even has a photo of Bloodworth with his autograph. He knew that Bloodworth was one of the top players on the Pirates, and he vaguely remembered that he had shoulder problems and had to retire in his mid-thirties. And he knew that Bloodworth was a highly paid player in the multi-millions. He was also aware that Bloodworth was active in trying to bring a triple-A baseball team to Nita City and had worked with others to have the Nita City Council support the effort. Bloodworth has talked with Westlake about his occasional work as a baseball scout, and Bloodworth has complained that his plans to be a baseball announcer or commentator were sidelined when he was falsely convicted of manslaughter a few years ago, when he was attacked by two men who were Phillies fans and called him and the Pirates a "bunch of pansies." Bloodworth told him they had all been drinking in a bar, and when they attacked him, he defended himself and landed a blow that apparently caused the guy to fall on the brass rail of the bar and the guy died. He said it was a bum rap, because he was in Philadelphia and the Pirates and Phillies hated each other, and when it went to trial a jury of Philadelphia fans "home-towned" him and found him guilty, and this ruined his career. Westlake said that Bloodworth wasn't worried because he invested his money well and didn't have to work. Bloodworth also told him that he had a "hot" girlfriend, but she needed to tone down her drug use.

Westlake said Fletcher has been a resident for over two years, since March of YR-4, and the only problem reported to Westlake has been Fletcher's alcoholism and occasional confusion about the location of his condo. On one occasion Westlake had to help Fletcher find his condo on the sixth floor when he was too drunk to find it. That was about two months ago, and Fletcher told Westlake that he had gotten lost before and once someone got angry because he tried the wrong door. Westlake did not know any more details about the incident. He did say that Fletcher drove a nearly new yellow Corvette, and said that recently the car had some front end damage and seemed to be missing part of the driver's side front fender, but Westlake knew nothing about how the damage occurred. Westlake took me out to the parking area in the back of the Plaza and showed me the car with damage to the front end. I took a photo of the car and labeled it Item # 9.

Westlake spoke with Bloodworth a day or two before November 7, and Bloodworth said someone took his billfold, and he was either going to get it back or someone was in trouble. Westlake asked how that happened, and Bloodworth said someone obviously got into his condo. Westlake asked if his condo was locked, and Bloodworth said he thought so. Westlake told Bloodworth it didn't make sense because their door locks were very expensive and secure and no one could break in or cause the tumblers to turn, and Westlake asked Bloodworth who he suspected of taking his billfold. Bloodworth responded by saying, "I don't have enough proof yet, but I'm going to find out."

Westlake heard later on November 7 that there were pills scattered on the floor after the burglary, and wondered whether there might be drugs involved. I informed Westlake that a few pills were on the floor, and asked if Westlake knew whether Fletcher had a drug problem. Westlake had no knowledge one way or the other. The only mention Westlake heard concerning drugs was what Bloodworth said about his girlfriend, and Westlake did not know the identity of the girlfriend.

I asked if Westlake knew of any other information about the background of either Fletcher or Bloodworth. Westlake said that when Bloodworth first made application for tenancy at Riverfront Plaza in January of YR-3, Westlake's office ran a background check and learned that Bloodworth had a criminal conviction for manslaughter, and when Westlake spoke with him about the matter, that's when Bloodworth related the facts of the incident. Westlake and the staff agreed that this should not present a problem at Riverfront Plaza. Westlake said in hindsight maybe they should not have accepted his application. Westlake asked that I not share that information with anyone as they wanted to avoid any civil suit ramifications. I explained to Westlake that I could not control the release of such information.

At the end of our conversation, Westlake added that Bloodworth and Fletcher had some contact with each other. When Westlake learned of the fight, Westlake remembered seeing them together in each other's condos, and said that Bloodworth used to come to Riverfront Plaza and visit Fletcher before Bloodworth actually moved into Riverfront Plaza. Westlake couldn't say which exact days, but it was multiple days that he visited Fletcher. Westlake thought it was a possibility that the two had a falling out and that Bloodworth might have suspected Fletcher stole his wallet and was meting out some punishment on November 7.

STATEMENT OF ELBIE GREENBERG:

On November 8, YR-2, at 1650 hours, I spoke with Greenberg, who is employed by the Nita City Fire Department as a paramedic. Greenberg and Whitey Gionfriddo of Medic 20 received a call from the Nita City Police dispatcher of a burglary suspect injured in the course of the burglary, and they responded to the Riverfront Plaza Condominiums yesterday morning. On my directions, they had searched Kenneth Fletcher, who appeared to be semiconscious, and determined his identity. They transported him to the Darrow County Medical Center. It appeared that Fletcher was drunk, and he was generally uncooperative during transport and following the arrival at the hospital. Greenberg searched his belongings at arrival and said that the only property on his person was his billfold, a set of key rings with a car device with a Corvette logo and a key, a set of sunglasses, and an iPhone bearing a sticker that appeared to be a return mail sticker with Fletcher's name and address. Additionally, Greenberg found three pills, which Fletcher claimed were his. The pills were not examined, but one was white and the other two were tan capsules. At the hospital, Fletcher demanded to be released, but medical personnel stated that Fletcher had received serious head injuries and insisted that he receive treatment and diagnostic tests. Greenberg said that Fletcher did not discuss what happened at the condo where he was injured, and they did not question him. Fletcher appeared very groggy throughout the ride to the hospital. Greenberg and Gionfriddo then left the Medical Center and returned to Medic 20 Station around 0400 hours. Greenberg said they did not retrieve the three pills, and they don't know what happened to them.

STATEMENT OF KENNETH FLETCHER:

On November 9, YR-2, at 1015 hours, I interviewed Fletcher in the Darrow County Medical Center. I informed Fletcher that he was suspected of entering Bloodworth's condo without permission with the intent to commit theft, there was evidence that he had taken pills from several bottles belonging to Bloodworth, and that Bloodworth struck him when Fletcher attacked him with a knife. I further advised him that he was not under arrest, as our investigation was proceeding, and that before we made any decision as to charges being filed we wanted to give him an opportunity to give us his side of the story. Fletcher said everything I told him about the evidence was a "bunch of bull." He said Bloodworth had invited him in for drinks after the two of them had earlier drunk beer together, sometime around 11:30 in the evening. During the evening, Bloodworth had called him a "mooch" and an "alky," and had made fun of him for losing his business. Fletcher told Bloodworth that if anyone was a has-been it's Bloodworth, who never was able to find work as a manager or coach or as a broadcaster after he quit baseball. Fletcher then told Bloodworth that he guessed they were both has-beens and they ought to just get along. Bloodworth bragged about how he would never have to work again because "he made millions." Bloodworth agreed they should get along and invited him to come by his place in an hour and he would give him some good Kentucky whiskey. Fletcher went to his own condo on the sixth floor, number 642, and about one hour later he went to the fifth floor and knocked on Bloodworth's door. Bloodworth told him he had a glass of sour mash and Fletcher held out his hand for the glass and told him that sounded good. Bloodworth suddenly hit him in the head. He said he remembers being hit several times and that's all he remembered until he was in the ambulance. Fletcher denied ever taking or even seeing pills at Bloodworth's condo and said the pills he had were his. He denied he used or even had a knife. I showed him the photo of the knife that Bloodworth turned over to me on November 7, and Fletcher emphatically denied ever seeing such a knife. He said I could ask anyone who knew him, and no one would ever be able to say they saw him with any kind of knife.

I asked if Fletcher had entered Bloodworth's condo a day or two before and taken Bloodworth's wallet, and Fletcher said "Absolutely not. I have never taken money or anything else from him or anyone else, and I have no need to. My business has definitely slowed down, and I cannot live the lifestyle that I had before the economy collapsed, but I can still live in comfort, and my real estate business is picking up." I asked Fletcher if he and Bloodworth had known each other, and if so, for how long. Fletcher said they had known each other for at least three or four years. I told Fletcher that Bloodworth said he did not know Fletcher, and Fletcher said, "Then he's a liar."

I asked Fletcher if he had a drinking problem. He said that it was not a problem, it was just something he had always done, and sometimes he drinks until he falls asleep. He said that since his divorce and since his realty business had dropped off, he had more time by himself and he probably had been drinking more lately.

Fletcher asked me when he could leave the hospital, and I told him he was not being held against his will, but the doctors said that he had a very serious head wound, and he should not leave until they gave him medical permission. I also told Fletcher that if he knew of any witnesses who could support his account of drinking earlier with Bloodworth and his being invited to Bloodworth's condo, he should notify me immediately so I could follow up with them. He said he thought he would be able to do that, but he had to talk to two Riverfront residents to see if they remembered drinking earlier.

I also asked Fletcher if he owned the Yellow Corvette with damage to the front end that was parked behind the Riverfront Plaza, and Fletcher said he did, but the damage was minor, and he planned to fix it soon. I asked him if he was recently experiencing financial problems, and he said that was not a problem, but he was cutting back somewhat on spending.

FURTHER INVESTIGATION:

In light of Fletcher's statement, on November 10, YR-2, I made several attempts at Riverfront Plaza to learn of individuals who may have been present when Bloodworth and Fletcher were allegedly drinking together the night of November 6 into the early morning of November 7, with negative results. No one was able to suggest who they thought would have been present. I again contacted Kerry Westlake, who was unable to suggest the names of any potential witnesses.

I also called Bloodworth and asked if he had the loose pills that were on the floor at the time of the fight, and he said that he did not. He threw them away since they were dirty.

FILE NUMBER: YR-2-29129

VICTIM: Kenneth S. Fletcher
4815 Riverfront Road #642
Nita City, Nita

SUSPECT: Gene Anthony Bloodworth

LOCATION: 4815 Riverfront Road #577
Nita City, Nita

OFFENSE: CC 245—Felonious Assault
CC 101—Murder

DATE OF REPORT: November 15, YR-2

BY: Detective Lee Howard
Badge Number 214

DETAILS OF OFFENSE:

FACTS:

See file number YR-2-29088 for initial factual details leading to the death of Kenneth Fletcher. Initial information the result of suspect's 911 call and statement led NCPD to believe that Fletcher was a suspect in the alleged burglary and assault with a deadly weapon involving Gene Bloodworth. However, supplemental investigation in that case included a statement by Fletcher, who stated that Bloodworth invited Fletcher to his condominium and that Bloodworth administered a beating to the drunken Fletcher. He also denied that he had a knife.

On November 13, YR-2, at approximately 1315, hours I was notified by NCPD and Dr. Tost of the Medical Examiner's Office that Fletcher had been released from the Darrow County Medical Center and three days later was found near his condominium in an unconscious state. He was determined by paramedics to have died, and the Medical Examiner's Office took possession of Fletcher's body. In my discussion with Dr. Tost, I asked that blood samples be taken to determine whether Mr. Fletcher's body revealed the presence of either alcohol or any drugs and was assured that they would do so. I also told Dr. Tost that we would need to take fingerprints from the body and that I would proceed to the morgue to secure both fingerprints and any other evidence on the body. At 1530 hours, I contacted Dr. Tost at the morgue and secured fingerprints from the body of Mr. Fletcher, which I marked as Item #9. I also took possession of his clothing and the Corvette keys, which I marked as Item #10. I later booked both items as evidence.

In a subsequent autopsy examination conducted by Forensic Pathologist Dr. Lou Tost of the Darrow County Medical Examiner's Office on November 14, YR-2, it was determined that Fletcher died as a result of the injuries he sustained at the hand of Bloodworth. Dr. Tost concluded that the cause of death was "blunt force trauma to the head," which was the result of the incident described in YR-2-29088. I spoke with Dr. Tost, who told me that Fletcher died from the head injuries he received on November 7, and there were no new, fresh injuries.

The supplemental investigation of the original burglary case included a statement from witness Billy Herman, who stated that Herman had seen Fletcher and Bloodworth together on at least two prior occasions, and there appeared to be friction or problems between the two. Herman said that Bloodworth used threatening words on one occasion, and on another occasion made a statement on a cell phone, that if directed to Fletcher would indicate animosity between the two.

After reviewing this case with Lt. Mulcahy, it was decided that this case should be treated as a possible murder case.

STATEMENT OF GENE BLOODWORTH:

On November 15 at 1415 hours, I contacted Bloodworth at his condo and informed him that our office was conducting further investigation in this matter. I told him that Mr. Fletcher had died and the autopsy surgeon confirmed that the cause of death was the beating that Bloodworth administered on November 7. I told him that I wanted to go over the statement that he gave on November 7, and I wanted to question him further. I told him that our office had made no final determination as to the matter.

I then reviewed Bloodworth's statement that he gave on November 7, and included in that account was his statement that he did not know Fletcher. When I finished reading that to him, he said, "That's it." I then confronted him with the information that Fletcher and Billy Herman provided about the two being together on two prior occasions, and Bloodworth then changed his story and admitted that he invited Fletcher to his condo. He said that he had Fletcher over, and they had been "hanging around." I asked Bloodworth if, in fact, Fletcher had left and then come back a second time with other individuals and they all were drinking, and he admitted that was true, but he did not remember who the others were. He also agreed that he had seen and been with Fletcher on a couple of occasions before that date. I mentioned to Bloodworth that Fletcher had recounted a conversation about Bloodworth's previous career with the Pirates, and Bloodworth denied any such conversation.

I informed Bloodworth that I had information that he and Fletcher had known each other for several years, that they had been in each other's condos on more than one occasion, and that Bloodworth had been in Fletcher's condo even before Bloodworth moved into Riverfront Plaza. Bloodworth said that was not true, and anyone who said that was either sadly mistaken or worse.

I informed him that our office had information that he had made threatening statements on a cell phone and we wanted to check the records of his cell phone, and asked permission to look at his phone. He said that he did not presently have a cell phone, as he turned his in to NitaCom for poor service and signals more than a month ago and has not purchased a new one. I informed him that a witness had seen him on a cell phone as recently as two weeks ago, and he said that he had borrowed the phone of a friend. I asked who the friend was, and Bloodworth refused to name the friend, saying he had no desire to involve anyone else in this matter.

I concluded the interview by informing Bloodworth that if he had any evidence pointing to his innocence, he would be well advised to pass that information on to our department before we concluded our investigation. He said that he had told us the truth and that was all he could provide. He said that it sounded like someone was trying to railroad him, and it begins to appear to him that the police now are buying someone's false story. He said that in light of the police questioning, he was going to talk to a lawyer and he had nothing further to say, except he did add one thing. He said that this was not the first time the police had falsely accused him when they made up a case of manslaughter and ruined his baseball career. He then got up and walked out of the interview.

FURTHER INVESTIGATION:

On November 15, YR-2, at 1530 hours, I called NitaCom and spoke with the Head of Security, Peter Castiglione, and I explained the issue about Bloodworth's use of the cell phone, and asked whether NitaCom could inform me of the status of Bloodworth's account and what information they were permitted to release concerning numbers he had called on his account. Castiglione informed me that NitaCom would call me back after checking records. At 1610 hours, Castiglione called me and stated that Bloodworth's account was closed on October 4, YR-2. According to their records, Bloodworth gave no explanation for closing his account. Castiglione stated that NitaCom could not release any called phone numbers without a court subpoena. Since Herman had stated the call was made approximately ten days prior to November 8, it did not appear that we would have a sufficient legal basis for seeking the NitaCom records of phone numbers called during the time frame Bloodworth had the cell phone.

I then secured Bloodworth's rap sheet and learned that he had been convicted of involuntary manslaughter in Pennsylvania following his conviction by a jury. He served two years in the State Correctional Institution at Mercer. I then obtained a copy of the Philadelphia Police Department report detailing the investigation of his case, which I have included in our departmental records of the present case. I then conferred with Deputy District Attorney James Bagby, who informed me that there was probable cause to arrest the defendant for murder. On November 23, YR-2, at 0800 hours, I returned to the defendant's condo and arrested him for a violation of Section 101 of the Nita Criminal Code. Bloodworth was booked into the Darrow County Jail. I advised him of his Miranda rights and he refused to discuss the case further on advice of counsel. Bail was set at $150,000. I was informed that bail was posted and at 1040 hours he was released.

EVIDENCE SEIZED AND BOOKED:

Item #9—One complete set of fingerprints from the body of Kenneth Fletcher, submitted for safekeeping to the Evidence Section.

Item #10—Two brown loafer shoes, one polo shirt, one pair of men's underwear shorts, one pair of what appeared to be golf socks, one pair of men's tan slacks, and a set of Corvette keys, all removed from the body of Kenneth Fletcher by Medical Examiner's staff, submitted for safekeeping to the Evidence Section.

FILE NUMBER: YR-2-29129

VICTIM: Kenneth S. Fletcher
4815 Riverfront Road #642
Nita City, Nita

SUSPECT: Gene Anthony Bloodworth

LOCATION: 4815 Riverfront Road #577
Nita City, Nita

OFFENSE: CC 245—Felonious Assault
CC 101—Murder

DATE OF REPORT: November 19, YR-2

BY: Detective Lee Howard
Badge Number 214

At 0845 hours, I continued further investigation into the backgrounds of both the defendant's and other witnesses' social media entries and statements relating to the relationship of Bloodworth and Fletcher.

I contacted the Riverfront Plaza Administrative Office and spoke to Art Herring, who informed me that his office would cooperate fully in our background investigation. He said that concern about the death of Fletcher had been raised by both residents of the Plaza as well as potential residents. As a result, the Plaza had urged residents to discuss the matter with his office, and they noted this in the Plaza's Facebook page. He also suggested that our office examine the Facebook pages of others, including Bloodworth's and Fletcher's Facebook pages. I thanked Herring for his cooperation.

I then obtained and examined the Facebook pages of Bloodworth, Fletcher, Billy Herman, the Riverfront Plaza, the Stag House Tavern, and the Nita City Council. I contacted the Philadelphia Police Department, and they sent me a copy of the Stag House Tavern Facebook page that they obtained and used in their trial resulting in Bloodworth's conviction. All of these pages were logged into our Evidence Section. I accessed the Nita City Council page and the Stag House Tavern pages, which are public pages that anyone can access; those of Bloodworth, Fletcher, and Herman I obtained by speaking with Kerry Westlake, who was "friended" by each of these residents of Riverfront Plaza. Westlake allowed me to see these personal pages through Westlake's Facebook account and to make copies of each page.

Item #11—A Kenneth Fletcher Facebook page copy, with latest date entered November 6, YR-2.
Item #12—A Billy Herman Facebook page copy, with latest date of October 5, YR-5.
Item #13—A Riverfront Plaza Facebook page copy, with latest date of November 18, YR-2.

Item #14—A Riverfront Plaza Facebook page copy, with latest date of September 8, YR-2.

Item #15—Mr. Bloodworth's Facebook page copy, with latest date November 4, YR-2.

Item #16—Stag House Tavern, Philadelphia, PA, with latest date August 23, YR-7.

Item #17—Nita City Council's Facebook page, with latest date November 15, YR-2.

NITA CITY POLICE DEPARTMENT
BUREAU OF IDENTIFICATION
FINGERPRINT ANALYSIS REPORT

FILE NUMBER: YR-2-29129

VICTIM: Kenneth S. Fletcher
4815 Riverfront Road #642
Nita City, Nita

SUSPECT: Gene Anthony Bloodworth

OFFENSE: CC 245—Felonious Assault
CC 101—Murder

DATE OF OFFENSE: November 7, YR-2

DATE OF EXAMINATION: November 17, YR-2

ITEM TO BE EXAMINED

Item #8—One 7-inch chrome plated knife, delivered to Latent Print Examiner Joan Russell by Detective Lee Howard November 17, YR-2.

Item #9—One set of fingerprints bearing the NCPD label "Fingerprints from the body of Kenneth Fletcher," delivered to Latent Print Examiner Joan Russell by Detective Lee Howard November 17, YR-2.

FINGERPRINT ANALYSIS

Item #8 was processed for prints on November 17, YR-5, by Latent Print Examiner Joan Russell, #3378, resulting in no legible prints. The knife appeared to be completely clean of any legible or smudged prints.

DISPOSITION

Items #8 and #9 were returned to the custody of Detective Lee Howard on November 17, YR-2.

Joan Russell, #3378
Latent Print Examiner
November 17, YR-2

PHILADELPHIA
POLICE DEPARTMENT

990 Spring Gardens Street
Philadelphia, PA 19123

MAJOR CRIMES INVESTIGATION REPORT

CASE #:	YR-7-174502
VICTIM:	Hugh Poland 9957 Foster Road Philadelphia, PA
SUSPECT:	Gene A. Bloodworth
OFFENSE:	PCC 2501—Murder
DATE:	August 22, YR-7
PREPARED BY:	Det. James Tabor, #1073

INVESTIGATION

I received a dispatch call at 0110 hours to proceed to the Stag House Tavern at 20955 Jackson Highway to investigate a reported fatality. I arrived at 0135 hours and was met by Officers Judd and Lakeman. They had the suspect, Gene Bloodworth, in custody. The on-scene officers also detained several witnesses to the altercation that led to the death of Hugh Poland. Mr. Poland was attended to by several witnesses, including the bartender, Jesse Levan, and Mr. Poland's two companions, Lou Finney and Jack Albright. Also detained was Eddie Basinski, a friend and companion of suspect Bloodworth.

Immediately after I arrived, the City of Philadelphia ER Team left in the ambulance with Mr. Poland and proceeded to Philadelphia General Hospital. At approximately 0230 hours, I was contacted by Philadelphia County Medical Examiner Investigator Rollie Hemsley, who informed me that Mr. Poland was dead on arrival at the hospital and the ME Office had taken custody of the body of Mr. Poland. I took statements from the five witnesses who had remained at the Stag House Tavern when I arrived.

At 0235 hours, I contacted CSI and requested that scene photos be taken and a scene diagram be prepared, and that any scene physical evidence including blood samples be preserved.

Statement of Jesse Levan

I interviewed Jesse Levan at 0245 hours at the Stag House Tavern. Mr. Levan stated the following:

Our business had slowed down when the altercation began. I was tending the bar. Our other bartender, Theresa Koecher, finished her shift at midnight. Most of our customers had left, and there were only two groups left. To my left, toward the back end of the bar, were three men. They were Hugh, who was a regular customer, and his two friends Lou and Jack. At the front end of the bar were the fellow you arrested and the guy with him who I understand is Eddie. I don't know his last name. They had arrived just after midnight, and the first thing they asked was whether we could put on the sports channel to find out the results of the Pirates and Giants game that was being played in San Francisco. The fellow you arrested, Gene, said they were from Pittsburg and had been to some kind of investment program, and it was time for a beer. Anyway, someone in the other group, I'm not sure who, but I think it was Hugh, said something like, "Go Giants." Well, that pretty well started the whole thing.

They kept to themselves pretty much until somebody on my right, I think it was the guy with Gene, Eddie, who said to Hugh, "Tell me, buddy, who are the lady horses playing? Then Hugh said, "Who are you talking about?" Then Eddie said, "You know, Phillies—that stands for lady horses." Then Hugh's friend Jack chimed in and said words to the effect, "And do you know what Pirates translated means? It means pansies!" That's when the guy you have in custody got up, put his beer down, walked over to the group and said, "They call me Guts. Who wants a piece of me?" Hugh then said something like, "Why don't we just all go home and forget this." Hugh put up his right hand, open hand style, with Guts about two to three feet away, and that's when this guy called Guts threw a punch and caught Hugh on the side of his head. Hugh went down, and I heard a loud thunk. His head hit the brass rail, and he just crumpled. I then saw blood coming out of his mouth, and we called 911. It took at least ten to fifteen minutes for the ER team to arrive, and when they checked his vital signs they said there were none. They gave him resuscitation. The ER team put him in the ambulance and left. I learned later that Hugh died.

I can tell you that Hugh was never obnoxious or violent. He was a friendly, non-violent guy who was liked by everyone. He had been a customer here for several years. This guy who calls himself Guts was a loudmouth Pittsburg jerk. I hope they execute him. I'm telling you now that I'll testify and so will the other witnesses. This was nothing but a callous murder.

Statement of Jack Albright

I interviewed Mr. Albright at 0310 hours in the Stag House Tavern. Mr. Albright stated the following:

Hugh, Lou and I get together once a month and go to a Phillies night game. Tonight we went to the Bank and watched the Phillies play the Cardinals. The Phillies won. We always go out after the game, usually to the Stag House, and have a few beers and talk about the game and baseball. We got there about 11:00 in the evening. We all felt pretty good. The Phillies won in the ninth inning on a walk-off home run. Sometime after midnight, we were sitting alone at the bar. These two guys came in. The taller guy with the loud voice, the guy who called himself Guts, he started talking about the Pirates. He was saying, the only team that counts in Pennsylvania is the Pirates. Pittsburg is the town that made steel. The Phillies play ball in a town that is full of little old ladies that go to tea parties. He said stuff like that. He said this stuff in a voice that was loud enough so everybody could hear it.

Well, several times we looked over, but Hugh kept saying, just ignore these guys. They obviously have been drinking too much.

Later on, Guts's friend looked over at us and said something about the Phillies being lady horses or something, and Hugh shot back something about the Pirates, I don't remember what. Lou and I told Hugh to shut up, these guys were trouble. We were right. Guts got up, walked over, thumped his chest, looked at us, and said something like, "Who's going to take me on?" Hugh said, "We're out of here. We're leaving," and he got up to go and Guts sucker punched him. Hugh never saw it coming. I've never seen anything like it. It was horrible. Hugh's head slammed back on the brass bar foot rail, and I heard this terrible sound. The next thing I saw was blood coming out of Hugh's head. This guy Guts had sort of a smug look on his face, and he just walked back to his beer and sat down and talked to his friend. They started to get up and Jesse, the bartender, told them not to leave. They were calling the cops. The two started to walk out, then turned around and came back while Jesse called 911. When Jesse got off the phone, I heard Guts say to his friend and to Jesse that all he was doing was defending himself and he claimed that Hugh started to punch him. That's a lie. And I promise Hugh and the police that I will testify to this.

Statement of Lou Finney
I interviewed Mr. Finney at 0335 hours in the Stag House Tavern. Mr. Finney stated the following:

By the time this whole thing happened, I was, as you might say, in my cups. I probably had too many beers, but fortunately I wasn't going to be driving. Hugh and Jack and I have been going to Phillies games for almost ten years. We were going back when they played in Veterans Park, and we have been going for a number of years in Citizens Bank Park. We always have a good time, but this time it was a great game and the Phillies pulled it out in the last inning. We had a beer or two at the park, and then when we got to Stag House we had several more. I probably drank more than they did. I remember these two guys coming in maybe a half hour or an hour before the fight. Well, it wasn't a fight. The big guy just cold cocked Hugh. I don't remember what was said before this happened. I know there was some small talk back and forth, and then nothing. No talk. Then someone said something about the Phillies, and then something was said about the Pirates, and the big guy walked over and said something and then hit Hugh. I don't even know whether Hugh was standing or seated, but I know Hugh didn't try and fight the big guy. I understand that they said Hugh died. I can't believe it. Over a baseball argument. This is going to destroy Hugh's family. His wife, his kids, his friends. I don't believe it.

Statement of Eddie Basinski
I interviewed Mr. Basinski at 0330 hours in the Stag House Tavern. Mr. Basinski stated the following:

I saw the whole thing. There were three drunks down at the end of the bar when Gene and I came into the bar. We had finished an investment seminar at the Choice Hotel and left the hotel and drove a short distance to the Stag House to have a beer. We planned on returning to the hotel, and then we were going to drive back to Pittsburg tomorrow. Anyway, we sat down at the bar and asked the bartender if he knew the Pirates score. They were playing the Giants on the West Coast, and so far as we knew, the game had probably just ended. The bartender said he was a Phillies fan and wasn't interested in changing the channel to get the Pirates score. I am a longtime Pirates fan, and I remember when Gene played outfield for them. He hurt his arm in winter ball and never was able to return to his old form, so he retired a little over a year ago. He was interested in investments. I'm a financial advisor and encouraged him to look into joining the industry. He had a well-known name in Pittsburg and could probably bring in clients. He agreed and we attended an annual seminar that American Standard puts on.

Well, one of the drunks made some kind of disparaging remark about the Pirates, and either Gene or I said something in response. That seemed to end it. But these guys kept drinking and getting louder. Then one of them said "the Pirates are a bunch of pansies." The remark was entirely gratuitous. We hadn't said anything. Gene said something like, "I'll take care of this. I'm going to cut it down. If they keep it up, we'll just go." He then walked over to them. I was carefully watching the whole thing. He said something I couldn't hear, and the guy he later hit got up, raised his right hand, and I thought he was going to hit Gene. Real quick, Gene hit him first and the guy fell down. Gene walked back to me and said that the guy tried to punch him and that's why he hit him. Heck, if I had been in his position, I would have done the same thing. I hope that you and the police department see it the same way. Gene is a gentleman and not a troublemaker, like those guys are. I'm awfully sorry what happened to the guy, but it wasn't Gene's fault.

Statement of Gene Bloodworth

After I had interviewed the above witnesses, at 0345 hours I interviewed Mr. Bloodworth. I did not advise him of the Miranda rights, as I was still investigating to determine who was at fault. He stated the following:

Eddie and I are old friends. We live in Pittsburgh. We came to Philadelphia to attend a seminar on operating a financial advisement service. Eddie has been in this business for some time, and he encouraged me to attend the American Standard Financial Services annual seminar held at the Choice Hotel. I have been retired from baseball now for about two years. I have spent some time scouting for the Pirates, the team I played on for six years. I was looking into something that would provide a steady source of income, and Eddie convinced me that I could learn financial advisement. The seminar began at 1:00 p.m. and recessed for an early dinner at 5:30, then reconvened at 7:00 p.m. It ended at 10:00. We went back to our hotel rooms, and Eddie suggested we go someplace besides the hotel bar, so we drove in his car to the Stag House Tavern. The hotel staff suggested the place, and it was close by. We got there around 11:30 or midnight, since we had a beer or two at the hotel bar before we left. When we got to the Stag House, it was pretty empty. The only other customers I saw were the three drunks at the other end of the bar. Right after we got there, I asked the bartender if he knew the score of the Pirates game. I got the impression right away that he didn't like the Pirates, and he said that no one was interested in that and left on some news show about women in bathing suits. It was okay, but the drunks at the other end of the bar started making loud comments about the Pirates. I told Eddie, "Let's go." Eddie said, "No. This is the only game in town for us. I want another beer." So we stayed. Then, more dumb comments from the drunks. They said the Pirates were a bunch of pansies. That's when I said, "You know what the Phillies are? Phillies stands for female horses." One of the drunks said something like, "Why is it that a bunch of female horses always beat the tar out of the pansies?"

Well, obviously looking back on it I should have kept my seat, but I thought, if I have to stay here and listen to this garbage, I want to put an end to it. I got up and walked over with the idea that I was going to be nice and suggest to them that we just be friends and forget the rivalry for one night. Without warning, the guy I hit got up, raised his right hand as if to hit me, and I punched him first before he could hit me. What happened after that was tragic, but, frankly, they brought it on themselves. All I did was defend myself, and I hit him only once before he clobbered me. I had a beer or two at the hotel, and I think I was on my second beer here when all this happened. Now I just want to go back to my hotel and get some sleep before I go home to Pittsburgh.

FURTHER INVESTIGATION

At 0415 hours on August 22, YR-7, I arrested Gene Bloodworth for a violation of Pennsylvania Crime Code Section 2501, unlawful homicide. He was taken to the Philadelphia City Jail at 0445 hours, where a blood sample was taken to determine the presence of any alcohol or drugs, and he was then booked. I was later advised that Mr. Bloodworth posted bail and was released at 0610 hours. Later that day at approximately 1510 hours, I spoke with Deputy District Attorney James Bagby, who had reviewed my investigation, and Deputy Bagby stated his office was filing a criminal complaint charging the defendant with a violation of PCC 2501 and he would be arraigned in court on August 26 at 9:00 a.m. in Department 16. He said that his office was assigning an investigator to conduct follow-up investigation, and said that he was sure the case would draw public interest, as that office had learned that Mr. Bloodworth was a well-known major league baseball player.

At 1310 hours on August 23, YR-7, I received a call from ME Investigator Hemsley that the autopsy of the body of Hugh Poland was conducted beginning at 0830 hours that date, and the autopsy surgeon, Dr. Richard Mauney, concluded that Mr. Poland died as a result of blunt force trauma to the left side of his head and the rear of his head, that there were two areas of hemorrhaging, but the direct cause of death was the severe hemorrhage at the rear as well as the fractured skull. Dr. Mauney concluded that there was no doubt the fatal injuries inflicted at the Stag House Tavern were the cause of death.

On August 28, YR-7, I was informed by the Crime Laboratory that the blood specimen taken from Gene Bloodworth on August 22, YR-7, contained 0.08 percent alcohol.

Prepared by Detective James Tabor on August 29, YR-7

CASE DISPOSITION

Mr. Bloodworth's jury trial began in the Court of Common Pleas before Judge John Wyrostek on March 15, YR-6. I was subpoenaed to appear and testify, which I did on March 19, YR-6. The jury trial concluded on March 22, YR-6, when the jurors returned a verdict of guilty of the lesser offense of involuntary manslaughter. The case was continued to April 20, YR-6, and on that day the court denied the defense request to place the defendant on probation, and Mr. Bloodworth was sentenced to State Prison for a term of three years. He was remanded to the custody of the Sheriff.

Prepared and added to original report by Detective James Tabor on April 21, YR-6

MEDICAL REPORTS

DARROW COUNTY MEDICAL CENTER
P. O. Box 16011
Nita City, Nita 85525

PATIENT: Fletcher, Kenneth S.
DOB: 02/14/YR-47
ACCT#: 0007781511

HISTORY AND PHYSICAL

DATE AND TIME OF ADMISSION: 11/07/YR-2, 5:10 a.m.

REASON FOR ADMISSION: Subdural hematoma, alcohol abuse.

HISTORY OF PRESENT ILLNESS: The patient is unable to give any history. He was drinking quite heavily. He was found breaking into someone else's condominium. He was assaulted and came in with a right temporal and nasal fracture. He was admitted to ICU. He is receiving Ativan for agitation.

PAST MEDICAL HISTORY: None except for alcohol abuse.

ALLERGIES: None known.

MEDICATIONS: None.

SOCIAL HISTORY: Patient lives in a condominium. He smokes and drinks copiously.

FAMILY HISTORY: Unclear, it appears he is divorced, has no family members nearby.

REVIEW OF SYSTEMS: Review of systems unobtainable. The patient is sedated.

PHYSICAL EXAMINATION: GENERAL: In bed in no acute distress.

VITAL SIGNS: Pulse rate 63, blood pressure 120/70, respiratory rate 13, afebrile.

HEENT: The patient has a distorted face, probably from multiple falls. He also has slight mild ecchymosis, with left temporal region and a right temporal region with no actual displacement or deformities I can see overtly. Pupils are equally round and reactive light.

NECK: Supple, good range of motion. No JVD.

HEART: Regular rhythm S 1-2.

LUNGS: Clear.

ABDOMEN: Soft, nontender. Show no clubbing, cyanosis, or edema.

LABORATORY DATA: White count is 4 with H and H of 14/539, platelets are 129. INR is 1.1, BUN and creatinine is 8/0.9, AST is 91, ALT is 83. Pro-BNP is 59. CPKs 230, MB is 1.7. LDH is 182. Ammonia level is 31. CT of the head shows displaced acute right nasal fracture, some right frontal temporal fragments. CT of the brain shows that he has an 8 mm left subdural hematoma probably contrecoup contusion. Blood ethanol level 0.216%, blood sample taken at 5:55 a.m.

IMPRESSION: A patient with alcohol abuse. The patient put on alcohol detox protocol. He has a subdural hematoma with some right temporal displacement. We will give him Keppra. We will start him on an insulin GI, DVT prophylaxis and watch for evidence of seizures. We will watch for signs of withdrawal seizures. Critical time spent on this patient is greater than 45 minutes.

Fritz Ostermueller, MD

DARROW COUNTY MEDICAL CENTER
P. O. Box 16011
Nita City, Nita 85525

PATIENT: Fletcher, Kenneth S.
DOB: 02/14/YR-47
ACCT#: 0007781511

DIAGNOSTIC IMAGING REPORT

EXAM: HEAT CT 11/07/YR-2 0845 hours.

CLINICAL INDICATION: 47-year-old male with subdural hematoma. The patient currently in ICU. He is argumentative, semiconscious, confused, and obviously intoxicated.

DICTATION DATE AND TIME: 11/07/YR-2, 0939 hours.

TECHNIQUE: Contiguous 5 mm cuts were obtained from the foramen magnum to the vertex without intravenous injection of contrast medium. Soft tissue and bone windows were obtained.

FINDINGS: Acute left-sided subdural hematoma approximately 8 mm in thickness. There is a mild mass effect but no midline shift. No subarachnoid hemorrhage or intracranial lesions. There is evidence of a questionable frontal orbital fracture.

The paranasal sinuses are clear.

Alicia Lyons
_____
Alicia Lyons, MD, Radiology

DARROW COUNTY MEDICAL CENTER
P. O. Box 16011
Nita City, Nita 85525

PATIENT: Fletcher, Kenneth S.
DOB: 02/14/YR-47
ACCT#: 0007781511

DIAGNOSTIC IMAGING REPORT

EXAM: CT BRAIN W/O CONTRAST (GN) 70450 11/08/YR-2

CLINICAL INDICATION: 47-year-old male with subdural hematoma. The patient is status post-alcohol withdrawal.

DICTATION DATE AND TIME: 11/08/YR-2, 0939 hours.

TECHNIQUE: Contiguous 5 mm cuts were obtained from the foramen magnum to the vertex without intravenous injection of contrast medium. Soft tissue and bone windows were obtained.

COMPARISON: Heat CT from 11/07/YR-2.

FINDINGS: In comparison to the prior study, there are no significant differences in the left anterior frontal convexity subdural hematoma which maximum thickness has slightly increased from 8 to 10 mm at this time. There is no evidence of significant mass effect on the surrounding brain parenchyma. There is also thickening of the subgaleal tissue in the left frontal region. There is no evidence of a midline shift. There is no evidence of subarachnoid hemorrhage. There is no evidence of an intracranial mass.

The bone windows do not display a fracture.

The paranasal sinuses are clear.

IMPRESSION: No major changes in left subdural hematoma.

Alicia Lyons
_____
Alicia Lyons, MD, Radiology

PATIENT: Fletcher, Kenneth S.
DOB: 02/14/YR-47
ACCT#: 0007781511

DISCHARGE SUMMARY

DATE OF DISCHARGE: 11/10/YR-2

DISCHARGE DIAGNOSIS: 1) Trauma with right subdural hematoma; 2) Status post-assault; 3) EtOH intoxication; 4) History of alcoholism.

DISCHARGE MEDICATIONS: Keppra 500 mg p.o. b.i.d. To continue routine home medicines, which was trazodone 1 to 1½ tablets daily, Paroxetine 40 mg p.o. daily, and Invega 6 mg daily.

HISTORY: The patient was brought into the emergency room by NCFD after consulting with NCPD. Apparently, he was intoxicated and went to the wrong condominium. When he entered the wrong condo in his complex, he was beaten by the person living there and the police officers were called. He was brought to the emergency room for evaluation and was found to have some altered level of consciousness as well as a left subdural hematoma. He was evaluated by neurosurgery. A repeat CT scan showed no change in the subdural hematoma. He was detoxified from his acute alcoholism and at this point in time is stable enough to be discharged home, with follow-up for a subdural hematoma from a neurology and resumption of his routine medications.

DIAGNOSTIC DATA: White blood count was 5.4, hemoglobin 14.3. Alcohol level is 216 on admission. Sodium was 133, potassium of 4.

CT scan showed no major change in left subdural hematoma on a repeat scan.

CONDITION ON DISCHARGE: Good. Fair prognosis pending any resumption of alcohol.

SOCIAL SERVICES COMMENTS: Social worker met with patient. He was aware of his discharge. Social worker called a taxi for him, and patient didn't feel he needed assistance. He stated that he would attempt to contact his ex-wife, but in any case, he could take care of himself. He planned to return to his condominium and to resume his normal work duties at Fletcher Realty. Social worker told patient he should avoid alcohol and not exert himself physically, and he should contact his family physician. Patient assured social worker he would do so.

Nicholas Strincevich, MD

Nicholas Strincevich, MD

OFFICE OF THE DARROW COUNTY
MEDICAL EXAMINER'S OFFICE
1865 Government Drive, Suite 101
Nita City, Nita 85523-2102
(204) 555-1101

AUTOPSY REPORT

Name of deceased: Kenneth S. Fletcher   **ME#:** YR 2-0712

Place of residence: 4815 Riverfront Road #642   **AGE:** 47 YEARS
Nita City, Nita

Place of death: 4815 Riverfront Road #642   **Sex:**   MALE
Nita City, Nita

Date and time of death (found):   November 14, YR-2: 0635 HOURS

Date and time of autopsy: November 14, YR-2; 1245 HOURS

CAUSE OF DEATH: BLUNT FORCE INJURY OF HEAD

OTHER SIGNIFICANT CONDITIONS: HEPATIC CIRRHOSIS

AUTOPSY FINDINGS:

I. Blunt force injury of head.

　　A. Decedent involved in a physical altercation that resulted in head trauma on November 7, YR-2; hospitalized November 7–10, YR-2 (see Medical Records).

　　　　i.   Found to have an acute left sided subdural hematoma (CT scan of the head from November 7, YR-2).

　　　　ii. Subsequent CT scan on November 8, YR-2, found no changes in the subdural hematoma.

　　　　iii. Blood ethanol level no admission to the hospital on November 7, YR-2: 0.216 percent.

　　　　iv. Decedent discharged in stable condition on November 10, YR-2.

　　B. Decedent found lying unresponsive in front of condo on November 13, YR-2. NCFD personnel examined decedent and pronounced death. Medical Examiner's Office, transported to the morgue.

　　C. Small faint contusions of the bilateral upper eyelids.

　　D. Fading contusion of the left side of the face surrounding the left angle of the mouth.

　　E. No subscalpular or subgalean hemorrhages or contusions.

F. No skull fractures.

G. Loosely clotted left-sided subdural hematoma (75 ml).

H. Neuropathology report.

    i. Left subdural hematoma with left to right cerebral midline shift.

        1. Subfalcine and central herniation with Duret hemorrhages in the pons.

    ii. Patchy subarachnoid hemorrhage.

II. Hepatic cirrhosis.

A. Prominent chronic inflammation of the portal tracts and fibrous bands.

B. Minimal steatosis.

III. Blunt force injury of torso.

A. Subcutaneous hemorrhage overlying the lateral fourth through sixth right ribs with recent healing fractures of the fourth and fifth lateral right ribs.

IV. Pulmonary congestion an edema (740 grams right lung, 640 grams left lung).

V. Fading contusions of the arms.

VI. Postmortem toxicology testing on antemortem blood (November 7, YR-2) negative for ethanol and common drugs of abuse (see separate Toxicology Reports).

Lou Tost, MD
_____
Lou Tost, MD
Forensic Pathologist
November 14, YR-2

AUTOPSY

WITNESSES: Forensic Autopsy Assistant Ralph Kiner.

IDENTIFICATION: The body is identified by a Medical Examiner's tag around the left big toe bearing the decedent's name and case number.

CLOTHING: The body is clothed in tan khaki pants, a sport shirt, tan socks, brown loafer shoes.

EXTERNAL EXAMINATION

The body is that of a normally developed and well-nourished man appearing consistent with the listed age of forty-seven years. The length is sixty-eight inches, and the weight is 157 pounds after removal of the medical therapy, gown and body bag. The body is unembalmed, well preserved, and at an ambient temperature. Rigidity is fully developed in the jaw and extremities. Lividity is posterior and blanches with pressure.

The scalp hair is brown with some gray. There is no balding. The irides are brown, the corneas clear, and the conjunctivae free of petechiae. The sclerae are non-icteric and free of hemorrhage. The ears are normally formed and located. The earlobes are creased. A 5/16 x 3/16-inch flat brown macule is just superior to the lateral edge of the left eyebrow. The nose is intact. There are no palpable fractures of the nasal cartilages. The lips are normally formed. The teeth are natural and fair condition. The frenula are intact. There is a small contusion of the right side of the upper buccal mucosa just lateral to the frenulum, and of the left side of the upper lip, described below. The facial bones are palpably intact.

The neck is straight and symmetrical.

The chest is normally formed and stable. The abdomen is flat and soft. There are no palpable masses. The external genitalia are those of a normal circumcised male adult, with both testes palpable in the scrotum.

The arms are normally formed and without deformities or palpable fractures. The axillae are unremarkable. No needle tracts or ventral wrist scars are noted. A 2-1/8 x 2-1/8-inch square patch is on the lateral right shoulder. It is labeled "Nicotine 21 mg/day." No ventral wrist or forearm scars are noted. The fingernails are relatively well groomed, with up to 1/8-inch overhang. The legs are normally formed and without edema, deformities, or palpable fractures. The back is straight and symmetrical. An 11 x ¼-inch vertically oriented surgical scar is on the left lateral chest just inferior and anterior to the axilla.

EXTERNAL EVIDENCE OF INJURY

A ¼ x 1/6-inch vertically oriented, linear dark red healing abrasion is just superior to the medial edge of the right eyebrow. A 3/8 x 1/8-inch horizontally oriented purple contusion is on the mid left upper eyelid. A ½ x 1/8-inch horizontally oriented faint red contusion is on the lateral aspect of the right upper eyelid. A 1¾ x 1¾-inch yellow contusion with overlapping purple discoloration is at the lateral angle of the left side of the mouth. A 1/8 x 1/8-inch very faint red-purple contusion is on the right side of the upper lip adjacent to the frenulum. There is fading red-purple contusion of the left side of the upper lip just lateral to the midline and along the vermilion border in a horizontal distribution, measuring ½ x 1/8-inch. There is a ¼-inch vertically oriented superficial red abrasion on the left side of the upper buccal mucosa, with possible surrounding faint contusion.

A 1¾ x 1¼-inch fading yellow-purple contusion is on the lateral right upper arm. A 1¼ x 3/8-inch horizontally oriented fading red-yellow contusion is on the proximal aspect of the posterior right upper arm. A possible 1 x ¾-inch extremely faint yellow contusion is on the left hip, with a pinpoint red abrasion or puncture within it. A ½ x ¾-inch focus of small purple-red contusions is on the right hip. A 2¾ x 1-1/8-inch vertically oriented light red-brown contusion is on the mid-dorsomedial left forearm. Proximal to this contusion is a possible 1¼ x 7/8-inch faint red-brown contusion. There do not appear to be any acute injuries of the hands.

INTERNAL EXAMINATION

BODY CAVITIES: The abdominal fat layer measures up to 3.3 cm in thickness. The body cavities do not contain any abnormal fluids. There are no adhesions. The serosal surfaces are smooth and glistening. The organs are normally positioned.

CARDIOVASCULAR SYSTEM: The heart weighs 340 grams and has an unremarkable shape with a smooth epicardial surface. The coronary arteries pursue a normal right predominant course and are widely patent, without appreciable atherosclerotic stenosis. The ostia are normally positioned and patent. The endocardium is intact, smooth, and glistening. The valves are normally formed, intact, and free of vegetations. The valve leaflets are thin and pliable. The fibrillar myocardium is red-brown, firm, and uniform without pallor, hemorrhage, softening, or fibrosis. The ventricles are not dilated. The right ventricular wall measures 0.4 cm in thickness, the left between 1.1 and 1.4 cm, and the interventricular septum 1.9 cm. The aorta follows its usual course and has fatty streaking to mild atherosclerosis of the abdominal aorta. There are the usual patent branches off of the aorta. There are no vascular anomalies or aneurysms.

RESPIRATORY SYSTEM: The right and left lungs weigh 740 and 640 grams, respectively. The pleural surfaces are smooth and glistening, with moderate anthracotic pigmentation. The lungs are congested and edematous. The lower lobes are discolored a deep purple. Cut surfaces vary from dark red to deep purple and are quite slick, exuding copious amounts of blood-tinged fluid. There is no gross consolidation, tumors, or enlargement of the airspaces. The bronchial mucosa is unremarkable and the pulmonary arteries are patent, without antemortem thromboemboli.

LIVER AND PANCREAS: The liver weighs 1490 grams. The capsule is intact. The liver is diffusely nodular. Cut surfaces are brown, firm, and nodular. There are no dominant nodules or other focal lesions. The gallbladder contains approximately 15 ml of thin, dark yellow-orange bile and no stones. The mucosa is intact and velvety, and the wall is thin and uniform. The pancreas has its usual shape and position. Sections are dark purple, lobulated, soft, and uniform. There is no gross fibrosis, calcification, or hemorrhage.

GASTROINTESTINAL SYSTEM: The esophagus and gastroesophageal junction are unremarkable. The stomach contains approximately 125 ml of bright to dark green fluid, with black particulate matter within. No pills, capsules, or fragments of food are identified. The gastric mucosa is intact. The pylorus is patent and the duodenum is intact. The small intestine is lined by a viscous film of tan fluid, except for the ileum, which contains bright yellow, somewhat seedy stool. The large intestine contains an abundant amount of soft non-watery brown stool. The vermiform appendix is unremarkable to inspection and palpation.

SPLEEN AND LYMPH NODES: The spleen weighs 270 grams. The capsule is smooth and intact. Cut surfaces are dark purple, firm, and uniform. There is no appreciable enlargement of the lymph nodes in the neck, chest, or abdomen. The intravascular blood is dark red, liquid, and abundant.

ENDOCRINE SYSTEM: The thyroid gland is not enlarged, and the lobes are symmetric. Cut surfaces are red-brown, firm, and uniform, without focal lesions. The adrenal glands have their usual shape and size. Sections reveal thin, uniform, yellow cortices and red-brown medullae. There are no tumors or hemorrhages. The pituitary gland is unremarkable.

UROGENITAL SYSTEM: The right and left kidneys weigh 160 and 170 grams, respectively. They have their usual shape and position. The capsules strip with some difficulty to reveal smooth cortical surfaces. Sections show the usual corticomedullary structure. The pelves and ureters are not dilated or thickened. The ureters flow their usual course to the bladder. The bladder is empty. The bladder mucosa is intact, though there are a few small bright red mucosal hemorrhages. The wall is not hypertropnhied. The prostate measures up to 4.3 cm in maximum cross-sectional diameter. Sections are tan to light yellow, spongy, and uniform, without focal lesions. The testes are unremarkable to external palpation.

NECK: The neck organs are removed en bloc with the tongue. No hemorrhages are seen in the strap muscles, thyroid, or pharyngeal constrictors. A 0.7 x 0.2-cm vertically oriented, linear streak hemorrhage is within the right side of the tongue. The cervical vertebrae, hyoid bone, and tracheal and laryngeal cartilages are without fracture. The airway is unobstructed and lined by smooth, pink-tan mucosa. There are light red petechial to slightly larger hemorrhages of the proximal tracheal mucosa. There is not displacement or crepitus of the cervical vertebrae. The atlanto-occipital joint is intact.

MUSCULOSKELETAL SYSTEM: There is focal red-purple subcutaneous hemorrhage within the fat overlying the lateral fourth through sixth right ribs. There are also patchy hemorrhages of the parietal surface of the lateral fifth and sixth right ribs. There are mildly displaced healing fractures of the fourth and fifth lateral right ribs, with a small amount of hemorrhage and focal small callus formation. There are no other fractures. There are no deformities. The ribs are not brittle. The skeletal muscle is dark red, firm, and uniform.

HEAD: Reflection of the scalp reveals no subgaleal or subscalpular hemorrhages. There are no skull fractures of either the calvarium or base of the skull. There is no epidural hemorrhage. There is approximately 75 ml of predominantly loosely clotted, though focally liquid, dark red subdural hemorrhage. The loosely clotted component is lightly adhered to the dura. The subdural hemorrhage is predominantly on the left side, though there is focal hemorrhage on the right. There do not appear to be any subdural neomembranes. The unfixed brain weighs 1070 grams. The leptomeninges are thin and transparent. There is patchy subarachnoid hemorrhage. The cerebral hemispheres are quite softened. The brain is placed in formalin for fixation and subsequent neuropathology examination.

TOXICOLOGY: Samples of central and peripheral blood, subdural blood, vitreous fluid, gastric contents, bile, liver, and urine from the reservoir are saved. The nicotine patch is also retained.

HISTOLOGY: Representative sections of organs and tissues are retained. Sections of the heart and liver are submitted for histology.

PHOTOGRAPHS: Multiple external and internal digital photographs are taken.

X-RAYS: Two x-rays of the head and chest do not demonstrate any prostheses, projectiles, or fractures.

EVIDENCE: Head hair is retained.

MICROSCOPIC EXAMINATION:

Heart: Two sections show perivascular fibrosis and occasional small foci of interstitial fibrosis. There is no myocardial inflammation or necrosis.

Liver: One section shows minimal patchy macrovesicular steatosis. There are bands of portal to portal bridging fibrosis with resultant nodule formation, consistent with cirrhosis. There is dense, predominantly chronic inflammation of the expanded portal tracts and fibrosis bands, and bile ductile proliferation within many of the portal tracts. There is focal spillage of the inflammation into the lobules.

LT/np
D: 11/14/YR-2
T: 11/18/YR-2

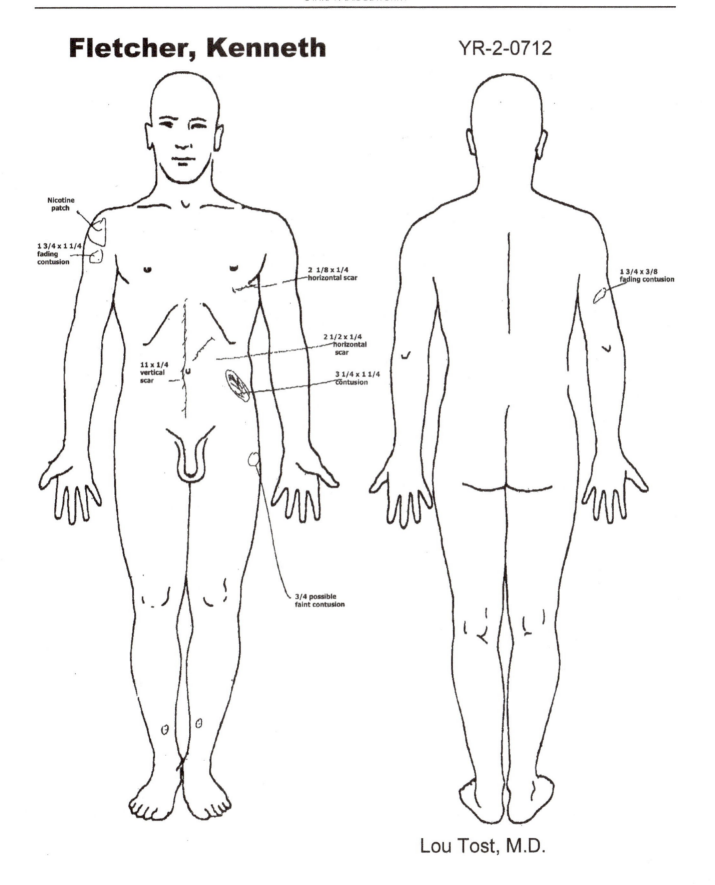

Fletcher, Kenneth

YR-2-0712

Nicotine patch

1 3/4 x 1 1/4 fading contusion

2 1/8 x 1/4 horizontal scar

2 1/2 x 1/4 horizontal scar

11 x 1/4 vertical scar

3 1/4 x 1 1/4 contusion

3/4 possible faint contusion

1 3/4 x 3/8 fading contusion

Lou Tost, M.D.

Fletcher, Kenneth

YR-2-0712

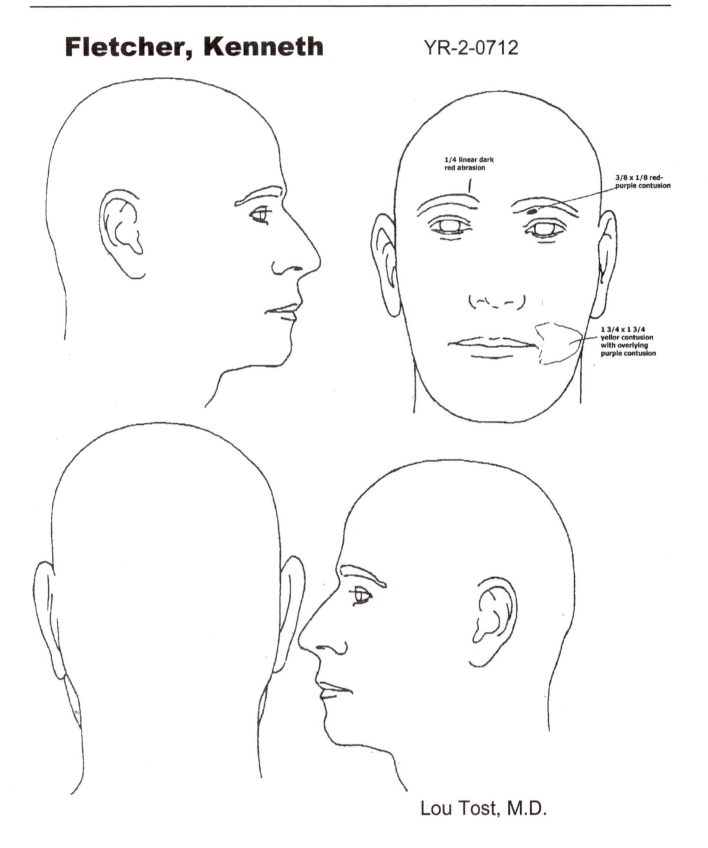

1/4 linear dark red abrasion

3/8 x 1/8 red-purple contusion

1 3/4 x 1 3/4 yellor contusion with overlying purple contusion

Lou Tost, M.D.

OFFICE OF THE DARROW COUNTY
MEDICAL EXAMINER'S OFFICE
LABORATORY OF FORENSIC SERVICES
1865 Government Drive, Suite 250
Nita City, Nita 85523-2102
(204) 555-1102

Dr. Lou Tost   LAB NO: YR-2-3090
Darrow County Medical Examiner's Office   AGENCY NO: YR 2-0712
1865 Government Drive, Suite 101
Nita City, Nita 85523-2102

NAME: Fletcher, Kenneth S. (victim)

TOXICOLOGY REPORT

Submission: 001   **Sample type:**   blood
Source: Lou Tost, MD   **Date received:**   November 15, YR-2

Assays performed:
barbiturates, benzodiazepines, benzoylecgonine (cocaine metabolite), methadone, methamphet-amine, opiates, phencyclidine.

Drugs confirmed:
None

Submission: 002   **Sample type:**   blood (antemortem)
Source: Lou Tost, MD   **Date received:**   November 15, YR-2

Ethanol Result: None Detected.

Kirby Higbe
Kirby Higbe   Date: November 19, YR-2
Supervising Criminalist

Arrest Records

ARREST AND CONVICTION RECORD OF GENE ANTHONY BLOODWORTH

RE: BAGBY, J. DDA DATE: 11-25-YR-2 TIME: 1630
CIR/D7184544
SEX/M
NAM/01 BLOODWORTH, GENE ANTHONY
NAM/02 BLOODWORTH, GENE aka GUTS
NDL/K5579353
SOC/695223566
****
ARR/DET/CITE/CONV:
#1
08-22-YR-7 ARR.PPD PCC 2501-MURDER
03-22-YR-6 JURY TRIAL-COURT OF COMMON PLEAS-CONVICTED PCC 2504-INVOLUN-
TARY MANSLAUGHTER
04-20-YR-6-COMMITTED TO STATE PRISON SCI-MERCER 3 YEARS
04-20-YR-4-RELEASED FROM CUSTODY ON PAROLE 1 YEAR
10-20-YR-4-DISCHARGED FROM PAROLE
****
#2
07-13-03 ARREST NCPD CC 23152(a)-DUI, MISDEMEANOR
07-15-03 RELEASED FROM CUSTODY, INSUFFICIENT EVIDENCE-B.A. 0.06%
****
ARR/DET/CITE/CONV:
#3
11-23-YR-2 ARR.NCPD CC101-MURDER, RELEASED ON $150,000 BAIL

NOT TO BE DUPLICATED

ARREST AND CONVICTION RECORD OF WILLIAM "BILLY" HERMAN

RE: BAGBY, J. DDA DATE: 06-14-YR-1 TIME: 1505
CIR/E4973134
NAM/01 SHERMAN, WILLIAM "BILLY" HERMAN
NDL/M3559791
SOC/747662121
****
LICENSE APPLICATION
#1
10-25-YR-10-APPLICATION FOR USED CAR DEALERSHIP LICENSE
11-15-YR-10-APPLICATION GRANTED, TERM 5 YEA RS, EXPIRES 11-15-YR-5
07-07-YR-07-PETITION TO REVOKE DEALERSHIP LICENSE FILED BY NDMV
07-30-YR-7-USED CAR DEALERSHIP LICENSE REVOKED
03-14-YR-4-USED CAR DEALERSHIP LICENSE RESTORED
****
ARR/DET/CITE/CONV:
#2
07-03-YR-7 CIT. NAG NVC 28051-ALTER INDICATED VEHICLE MILEAGE,
MISDEMEANOR
07-29-YR-7 CONVICTION, MISDEMEANOR NVC 28051, MISDEMEANOR, 2 YEARS
PROBATION, RESTITUTION, FINE $5,500

NOT TO BE DUPLICATED

ARREST AND CONVICTION RECORD OF SADIE ALLISON McLISH

RE: BAGBY,J. DDA DATE: 11-11-YR-1 TIME: 1458
CIR/B7653449
NAM/01 McLISH, SADIE ALLISON
NAM/02 McLISH, SADIE THE STOKER
SOC/535017849
****
ARR/DET/CITE/CONV:
#1
07-08-YR-14 ARREST DCSD C.C. 11357(c) POSSESSION OF MORE THAN 28.5 GRAMS OF MARIJUANA, MISDEMEANOR
07-27-YR-14 PETITION SUSTAINED, JUVENILE COURT, INFORMAL SUPERVISION, 1 YEAR PROBATION,
****
#2
04-07-YR-11 ARREST NPD, C.C. 11350, POSESSION OF HEROIN, FELONY, RELEASED & HOSPITALIZED SOUTHBURG CENTRAL HOSPITAL
05-15-YR-11 GRANTED DIVERSION FOR 2 YEARS, CONDITIONS: ATTEND & COMPLETE DRUG PROGRAM OF DARROW COUNTY, SUBMIT TO SEARCH & SEIZURE, NO FURTHER VIOLATIONS.
05-25-YR-9 DIVERSION COMPLETED, C.C. 11350 DISMISSED
****
#3
11-10-YR-4 ARREST NCPD CC 23152(a)-DUI, MISDEMEANOR
11-22-YR-4 CONVICTED, PLEA OF GUILTY, MISDEMEANOR DUI: SEN. 3 YEARS FORMAL PROBATION, 2 DAYS COUNTY JAIL, FINE $750
****
#4
04-03-YR-2 ARREST NPD CC 647(f)-PUBLIC INTOXICATION, MISDEMEANOR
04-27-YR-2 CONVICTED, PLEA OF GUILTY, MISDEMEANOR CC 647(f): SEN. 1 YEAR SUMMARY PROBATION, FINE $347

NOT TO BE DUPLICATED

ARREST AND CONVICTION RECORD OF CHRIS SINGLETON

RE: BAGBY, J. DDA DATE: 11-11-YR-1 TIME: 1515
CIR/D9428731
NAM/01 SINGLETON, CHRIS
NDL/M7882929
SOC/25586414
****
ARR/DET/CITE/CONV:
#1
03-13-YR-5 CIT. NDA CC 484-GRAND THEFT, FELONY
04-14-YR-5 PLEA NO CONTEST, CONVICTION, MISDEMEANOR CC 487, THEFT BY FALSE PRETENSES, 2 YEARS PROBATION, 1 YEAR COUNTY JAIL, SUSPENDED, RESTITUTION PURSUANT TO CIVIL JUDGMENT, FINE $10,000

NOT TO BE DUPLICATED

ARREST AND CONVICTION RECORD OF KENNETH S. FLETCHER

RE: BAGBY, J. DDA, DATE: 12-28-YR-2 TIME: 1630
CIR/E7693466
DOB: 02-14-YR-47
SEX: M
NAM/01 FLETCHER, KENNETH S.
NAM/02 FLETCHER, STEWART K.
NDL/C5477929
SOC/431078125
****
ARR/DET/CITE/CONV:
#1
04-24-YR-22 ARREST DCSD C.C. Y & C.C. 647(f), PUBLIC INTOICATION, MISDEMEANOR
05-27-YR-22 PLEA GUILTY C.C. 647(f), MISDEMEANOR, 1 YEAR SUMMARY PROBA-
TION, OBEY ALL LAWS, NO ALCOHOL
****
#2
02-04-YR-21 ARREST NCPD C.C. 415-DISTURBING THE PEACE, MISDEMEANOR &
C.C. 647(f) PUBLIC INTOXICATION
03-13-YR-21 PLEA OF GUILTY TO C.C. 415-DISTURBING THE PEACE, MISDEMEANOR,
2 YEARS INFORMAL PROBATION
****
#3
07-15-YR-15 ARREST NCPD C.C. 23152(a)-DUI, MISDEMEANOR
07-28-YR-15 CONVICTED, PLEA OF GUILTY, MISDEMEANOR DUI: SEN: 3 YEARS
INFORMAL PROBATION 3 YEARS, 2 DAYS COUNTY JAIL, FINE $540
****
#4
09-06-YR-7 ARREST DCSD C.C. 476a-INSUFFICIENT FUNDS CHECKS, MISDEMEANOR
12-15-YR-7 DIVERSION GRANTED, 18 MONTHS, CONDITION NO VIOLATIONS.
06-15-YR-6 C.C. 476(a) DISMISSED
****
#5
08-31-YR-5 ARREST DCSD C.C. 273.5-SPOUSAL ABUSE
10-07-YR-5 DIVERSION GRANTED, 2 YEARS, CONDITION NO VIOLATIONS
10-10-YR-3 C.C. 273.5 DISMISSED
****
****
#6
04-15-YR-3 ARREST NCPD CC 647(f)-PUBLIC INTOXICATION, MISDEMEANOR
CONVICTION, PLEA OF GUILTY TO C.C. 647(f)-PUBLIC INTOXICATION, 1 YEAR
SUMMARY PROBATION, 40 DAYS COUNTY JAIL N

NOT TO BE DUPLICATED

PRELIMINARY HEARING TESTIMONY

TESTIMONY OF DETECTIVE LEE HOWARD AT PRELIMINARY HEARING[1]

Direct Examination

My name is Lee Howard. I am a detective with the Nita City Police Department. I have been employed by NCPD for sixteen years. I served six years in Patrol, two years in Internal Affairs, and eight years in Detectives. During those years I have worked a variety of cases including homicides, robberies, burglaries, other crimes of theft, and crimes against the person, such as assaults, batteries, child molestation, and rapes.

I participated in the investigation involving the death of Kenneth Fletcher beginning first on November 7, YR-2, when I was the on-call detective that early morning. Shortly after 2:00 a.m., I received a call from Dispatch informing me that Lt. Mulcahy had assigned me to a residential burglary at the Riverfront Plaza Condominiums that was in progress and patrol officers had been directed to respond. I actually arrived at the scene before any patrol officers. I contacted the defendant at his condo on the fifth floor. Officer Roe arrived very shortly after I got there. I saw Kenneth Fletcher lying on the floor and he appeared to be unconscious. I spoke with the defendant, who told me that Fletcher had broken into his condo, woke him up, and tried to kill him with a knife. He said that Fletcher either must have been trying to find money or drugs, and pointed to pills and pill bottles on the floor. The defendant said he had to protect himself, and he punched Fletcher several times, knocking him out.

At no time did the defendant ever refer to Fletcher by name. He said the first time he knew that Fletcher had a knife was after he knocked him to the floor, and then he saw the knife on the floor. He pointed out the knife, which was on a small table near the front door. He then told me that the 911 operator told him to pick up the knife and put it in a safe place so that the burglar could not get it, and the defendant placed it on the table. I first photographed the knife in its position on the table, and then I took possession of the knife, and carefully, without placing my hands on the knife, I placed it in an evidence envelope. Later, I booked both the knife and the photo in evidence. Exhibit 2 for Identification is the photo of the knife, and it accurately shows its appearance as I found it. Exhibit 3 for Identification is a photo of the knife at police headquarters showing the knife with its blade open next to a ruler. Exhibit 4 for Identification shows Fletcher in an unconscious state lying between the dining area and the kitchen near a blood spot and three pills, and Exhibit 5 for Identification is a close-up view of the same. Exhibit 6 for Identification shows the three pill bottles and some scattered pills near the doorway to the master bedroom. And Exhibit 7 is a diagram I secured from the Riverfront Plaza Condominiums that shows the floor plan of unit number 577, and I have added the location of Fletcher, the table with the knife, and the location of the pills. Each accurately depicts these items and events as I saw them that early morning.

The medics from the Nita City Fire Department arrived shortly after, and they began to treat Fletcher, who had begun to partially regain consciousness. He appeared to be seriously injured and intoxicated. He had blood on his face and there was blood on the floor. The Fire Department personnel

---

[1] The transcript of Detective Lee Howard's testimony was excerpted so that only Detective Howard's answers are reprinted here. Assume that this is a true and accurate rendering of Detective Howard's answers. The testimony was given at the preliminary hearing on July 20, YR-1, in the Darrow County Municipal Court, Nita City, Nita.

informed me that Fletcher needed immediate treatment and hospitalization, and I authorized them to take Fletcher to the Darrow County Medical Center.

I did not formally arrest Fletcher. My reasons included his serious injury and a lack of certainty in my mind about the accusations the defendant made. I then believed that more investigation was necessary. One of the factors was that I observed no evidence of any forcible entry into the defendant's condo. And the defendant had told me he believed that his front door was locked. Also, I never found any evidence that Fletcher had a key that would work for the defendant's front door.

On November 14, I was advised by Dr. Lou Tost that Fletcher died on that day as a result of injuries including a subdural hematoma that the defendant caused by beating Fletcher, along with complications of cirrhosis of the liver. Dr. Tost informed me that Fletcher had been found lying unconscious outside his condo, and when emergency medical personnel arrived, they determined that he was dead. The Medical Examiner's Office was then advised, and they took over the case. Fletcher's body was transported to the Darrow County Morgue. I requested that in the investigation as to the cause of death, the Medical Examiner's Office or the medical examiner secure both blood samples and fingerprints from Fletcher's body. At that time, I conducted an active homicide investigation.

On November 15, I interviewed the defendant at his residence in the Riverfront Plaza Condominiums about 1400 hours. He was not under arrest, and I told him that I was following up on our investigation into the alleged burglary of his residence, and I advised him that Fletcher had died as a result of the injuries he sustained in the fight on November 7. Mr. Bloodworth told me he did not know that. I did not advise him of any Miranda rights, as I was still investigating and I had not determined several aspects where Fletcher's account and that of the defendant varied.

The first thing I did was to advise Bloodworth what I understood was his account, and I did this by reading back my notes of my conversation with him on November 7. I told him that he had said he was asleep in his bedroom, he woke up to a noise, he saw a male standing in the doorway, and he yelled, "What the hell are you doing here?" He had said that when the man came toward him, he jumped out of bed and they started fighting. Fletcher was swinging and missing, and Bloodworth punched him a couple of times, forcing him into the dining area. He had said that Fletcher swung at him some more, and Fletcher was off balance, and suddenly the defendant saw a light from outside glare off something in his hand. The defendant said he had then hit Fletcher a couple more times, knocking him out. While Fletcher was lying on the floor, the defendant had called 911 and told them what happened. Then he had seen the knife in Fletcher's hand and told the 911 dispatcher, who told him to get it away. Then the defendant kicked the knife away. The defendant had said that medications were on the floor, and Fletcher must have taken them from the back of his condo and dropped them.

He had said that he had seen Fletcher before in the complex but didn't know who he was, and said he thought he might live there. The defendant told me that two nights before, someone had broken into his condo and stolen his wallet. He said he was pretty positive he had locked the door and didn't know if Fletcher had a key. After I read those notes to him, the defendant said to me, "That's it. There's nothing more." The person I have identified as the defendant, Mr. Bloodworth, is sitting at counsel table in the dark blue suit.

COURT: The record will reflect that the witness has identified the defendant Gene Bloodworth.

I had received information in my investigation that witnesses had seen Bloodworth and Fletcher together previously, so I pursued that point and the defendant then said that he had Fletcher over, and they had been "hanging around." I asked the defendant if in fact Fletcher had left and then come back a second time with other individuals and they all were drinking, and he admitted that was true. I then asked him if there had been a discussion between the two of them about baseball and Bloodworth's past career, and he didn't recall any particular topics they may have talked about.

I told the defendant that our department had information that the two of them had been seen together in the past in each of their condos dating back to before the defendant moved to the Plaza. The defendant at that time seemed to grow angry, and said that whoever said that was lying. At that time, the defendant said this whole investigation was "a railroad job," but that didn't surprise him because he had been railroaded before by police. He said he was sorry he ever cooperated with the police, and from now on he was going to cooperate with one person, and that was the lawyer that he was going to hire. The defendant then got up and walked out, leaving me standing in the living room of his condo. I then picked up my note pad and left, closing the door. I went promptly to the manager's office and informed the staff that I had left condo number 577, and asked them to lock the door as Bloodworth had left it unlocked.

I had also been informed that witnesses who knew Fletcher said he had never displayed any aggressive tendencies, and they found the defendant's accusations that Fletcher burglarized the defendant's condo and attacked him with a knife to be "totally unbelievable."

COURT'S RULING ON OBJECTION: Defense counsel objected to the court considering what others said about the alleged statements made about Fletcher never displaying aggressive tendencies as impermissible hearsay. The court ruled that the evidence would not be admitted for the truth of the matter, but the evidence would be allowed solely on the issue of why Detective Howard continued to investigate the case further.

It was very clear to me that the defendant was not being square with me. He was contradicting people who had no axe to grind in this case. I informed Lt. Mulcahy that I believed we had a homicide case, and I was directed to pursue the case. I then conferred with Deputy District Attorney James Bagby, who informed me that there was probable cause to arrest the defendant for murder. On November 23 in YR-1, I returned to the defendant's condo and arrested him for a violation of Section 101 of the Nita Criminal Code. I advised him of his Miranda rights, and he said he had no intention of discussing the case further with our department, and if I wanted any information, I could just contact his attorney. I asked who his counsel was, and he said he was in the process of selecting an attorney. I concluded my discussion with Bloodworth at that time.

Following his arrest, I continued to investigate whether there were any social media discussions that bore on this issue. I was able to confer with the Riverfront Plaza Administration Office, and they directed me to their public website and I received their permission to retrieve both Facebook pages. The page describing the Plaza and making reference to the recent death of Fletcher is Exhibit 12, and the page relating to the previous party that both Fletcher and Bloodworth attended is Exhibit 13. I then contacted the Philadelphia Police Department and they sent me a copy of the Facebook page of the Stag House Tavern, the site of the death of Hugh Poland, leading to Bloodworth's conviction for involuntary manslaughter in YR-7, which is marked Exhibit 15. I was advised by the Plaza's

Administrative Office to contact their manager, Kerry Westlake, to see if Westlake was permitted by any of the Plaza residents to be Facebook friends, and if so, whether they would permit me to view their Facebook pages for matters related to the death of Fletcher. On the afternoon of November 23, I spoke with Kerry Westlake, who told me that Fletcher, Herman, and Bloodworth each had listed Westlake as a Facebook friend and permitted me to review their pages and to make copies of any of those pages. I did this for the defendant's Exhibit 14, for Fletcher's Exhibit 10, and for Herman's Exhibit 11. Finally, the Nita City Council Facebook page is a public Facebook, and Exhibit 16 from that page relates to the defendant.

COURT'S RULING ON OBJECTION: Defense counsel objected to the court allowing both the testimony and all Facebook exhibits except Exhibit 16, and the court ruled that Exhibits 10 through 16 were admissible and the testimony relating to each exhibit was also admitted.

Cross-Examination

The defendant was cooperative at all times, from the time that I first encountered him in his condo until I had mentioned that he and Fletcher had been seen together in their condos on previous occasions. I did not contact any people other than those mentioned in the police reports concerning whether they had witnessed Fletcher and the defendant together on previous occasions. In my two interviews with the defendant, I did not tape record our conversations, but I did take detailed notes that I subsequently used in preparing the reports. And, no, I don't still have those notes. Once I wrote the reports, I destroyed the notes. In my opinion, that is in full compliance with departmental procedures.

I did not go door-to-door throughout the Riverfront Plaza to conduct, as you call it, a scene canvass for further witnesses other than my effort to do so the early morning when Fletcher was taken to the hospital. But on that occasion, I did go door-to-door on the fifth floor, and of the ten to twelve on that floor, only three or four answered the door, and no one had heard or seen anything.

I did not conduct a search of Fletcher's condo at any time, so I cannot say whether he had the wallet of the defendant, or whether he had any knives, any drugs, or any other evidence that might relate to the incident of November 7. And I did not contact any witnesses to see if Fletcher had entered their condos, or if they had seen Fletcher use drugs. I did not book as evidence any of the drugs on the floor of the defendant's condo. No, I did not check to see if pills recovered by Greenberg were the same as those in the pill containers on the floor. No, I did not have those pill containers checked to see if Fletcher's prints were on the containers, and I did not book them as evidence.

I did not interview Bloodworth's girlfriend, and in fact, I have no knowledge of her identity. In my investigation, I did not find any witnesses who testified that they had ever seen the defendant act with violence. But I certainly am aware of a prior case where the defendant was convicted of manslaughter (objection overruled). I did not check to see if Fletcher had funds in the bank, and I did not check with his former wife or friends to see if he had any severe money problems or financial needs.

I did not check with Fletcher's friends, people he worked with, or former business associates to determine what his character for violence was. I do know from working cases both as a detective and as a patrol officer that some people who are ordinarily law abiding and peaceful can become combative and assaultive when they are drinking. I did learn that Fletcher was found by the autopsy surgeon to have a condition described as hepatic cirrhosis, and I do understand that such a condition is consistent with longtime alcohol and/or drug abuse. I also learned that there is evidence that Fletcher may have either entered condos belonging to other people or attempted to do so when he was possibly drunk.

I do understand that the law of the State of Nita allows people to use necessary force to protect themselves from others who invade their homes. That's why I wrote up the original report as a possible burglary and felonious assault. I don't disagree that Bloodworth had a right to defend himself if, in fact, Fletcher entered Bloodworth's condo around 2:00 a.m. without permission and threatened Bloodworth with great bodily harm or death.

I hereby certify that the foregoing is a true and correct transcription of the testimony of Detective Lee Howard on July 20, YR-1, at the preliminary hearing in *State v. Bloodworth*, in the Darrow County Municipal Court, Nita City, Nita.

Certified by:

Culley Rikard

CULLEY RIKARD
Court Reporter

TESTIMONY DR. LOU TOST AT PRELIMINARY HEARING[2]

Direct Examination

I hold a medical degree and am a pathologist and Director of the Pathology Laboratory of the Darrow County Medical Examiner's Office here in Nita City. I graduated from Nita University with a BS in Biology in YR-16. I received an MS degree in Biology at Southern Methodist University in YR-14. In YR-11, I earned an MD from Case Western Reserve University. I was a resident in Anatomic and Clinical Pathology at Duke University Medical Center from YR-11 to YR-8. I then served as an Assistant Chief Medical Examiner in Chapel Hill, North Carolina, for one year as a part of a forensic pathology fellowship. I became a forensic pathologist with the Diagnostic Pathology Medical Group in Nita City. In YR-6, I accepted a position as Assistant Director of Pathology at the Darrow County Medical Examiner's Office. Three years later, I was appointed as the Director. I have taught pathology at Nita University Medical School from YR-5 through YR-2 and at the University of Southern Nita Medical School, from YR-2 to the present. I am board certified in three fields of pathology: anatomical, clinical, and forensic. I also sit regularly on the Certification Board of the American Board of Pathology as an examiner of applicants for board certification. I have testified in state and federal trial courts in this state and in North Carolina and given expert testimony in the field of forensic pathology on approximately 110 occasions. On most such occasions, I was called by the prosecution, but in at least fifteen cases, I was called to testify as a defense witness.

In the course of my work in North Carolina with Diagnostic Pathology Medical Group and for the Darrow County Medical Examiner's Office, I have performed over 2,000 autopsies. Of those autopsies, at least 15 percent were classified as death by blunt force to the head. I would estimate that at least 5 percent involved findings of hepatic cirrhosis. I have qualified as an expert and testified in court and rendered opinions with respect to blunt force trauma or injury to the head on more than twenty occasions. I have lectured in the field of blunt force injury to the head before groups of doctors, police officers, medical staff of hospitals, and have taken part in professional group discussions in this area. Exhibit 8 for identification is a current copy of my professional resume and accurately states in summary my professional background and experience.

On November 13, YR-2, I was informed at the Darrow County Medical Examiner's Office by Investigator Gene Woodling that Kenneth Fletcher had been discovered lying directly outside his condo at the Riverfront Plaza Condominiums and was declared dead by emergency medical personnel. Investigator Woodling arrived at the scene, took custody of the body, placing it in a body bag, and returned with the body to the Medical Examiner's Office, where it was placed in the morgue. Later that day, Detective Howard, with my permission, took a full set of fingerprints and Mr. Fletcher's clothing. At Howard's request, I took a vial of blood from Mr. Fletcher's body, sealed it, and had our laboratory analyze it for the presence of alcohol or drugs.

I performed a general autopsy examination on the body of Kenneth Fletcher at the Darrow County Medical Examiner's Office on November 14, YR-2, at approximately 8:30 a.m. Kenneth Fletcher

---

[2] The transcript of Dr. Lou Tost's testimony was excerpted so that only Dr. Tost's answers are reprinted here. Assume that this is an accurate rendering of Dr. Tost's answers. The testimony was given at the preliminary hearing on July 20, YR-1, in the Darrow County Municipal Court, Nita City, Nita.

was forty-seven years old, five feet seven inches long, weighed 147 pounds, and had brownish hair and brown eyes. During my external examination of the body, I observed a dark red abrasion above his right eyebrow, a red-purple contusion immediately below his left eyebrow, and a yellow contusion with an overlying purple contusion immediately left of his mouth. I observed multiple contusions about his body; there was a fading contusion on the front of his right upper arm and another to the back of the same arm. He had a larger contusion, measuring three-and-one-quarter-inch by one-and-one-quarter inch, on the left side of his abdomen. I also observed what I describe as three-quarter-inch possible faint contusion at the left hip. So, in total, six contusions and one abrasion. An abrasion is a wound generally caused by superficial damage to the skin. A contusion is a bruise, a minor hematoma, where usually capillaries are damaged by trauma allowing blood to seep into surrounding tissues. These injuries all appeared consistent with occurrences approximately six days prior to death.

I next performed an internal examination, and I found no evidence of any factors that would contribute to the cause of death other than a left subdural hematoma producing brain swelling and herniation. Brain herniation is a deadly side effect of very high intracranial pressure that occurs when the brain shifts across structures within the skull. Herniation can be caused by a number of factors, including traumatic brain injury, stroke, or brain tumor. In this case, I found no evidence of either a stroke or a brain tumor. Because such herniation puts extreme pressure on parts of the brain thereby cutting off the blood supply to parts of the brain, it is often fatal.

I also found a subcutaneous, or beneath the skin, hemorrhage above the rib area along with recent healing fractures of the fourth and fifth lateral ribs, and these would not have been fatal injuries. All the injuries I have described are consistent with Mr. Fletcher suffering a beating on or about November 7, YR-2. In my opinion, Mr. Fletcher died as a direct result of blunt force trauma to the head, which produced the fatal subdural hematoma.

It is true that Mr. Fletcher also displayed evidence of hepatic cirrhosis, which is a consequence of chronic liver disease. That condition is most commonly caused by alcoholism, but there are many other possible causes. While that condition existed, in my opinion it did not cause his death, which was solely the direct result of the trauma and the resulting subdural hematoma.

Cross-Examination

There is no official certification one can acquire to become an expert solely in blunt force trauma to the head. There are no specific courses given in medical school dealing specifically with this area. However, great attention is given and emphasis placed on this topic during forensic pathology fellowship training. It is one of the significant causes of death, and, therefore, in my field of practice, it is a subject of considerable study.

It is true that one can experience blunt force trauma to the head from a variety of causes, including falling, accidentally bumping the head against a hard object, or being involved in other types of accidents. It is also true that people who are chronic alcoholics can suffer such accidents when they are under the influence of alcohol. My practice has included the study of the effects of alcohol on the human body and mind, observing individuals in various stages of intoxication, correlating their behavior with blood alcohol levels, and on occasion testifying in court concerning my findings and conclusions in individual cases. I have been found by courts to be an expert in this field on at least four occasions. And, it is true that Mr. Fletcher's blood alcohol level when his blood was tested on November 7 was found to be 0.216 percent. That is more than two-and-one-half times the amount at which all people are found to be unsafe drivers. At his level of intoxication, most people would experience significant impairment of judgment, of visual acuity, of physical coordination, of balance, and general perception of events. It is also not unusual for one who generally has an even disposition and temper to become combative and violent when under the influence of alcohol. I have seen this change in behavior in many individuals and have read definitive studies in the field substantiating this.

I am familiar with the concepts of absorption and dissipation or metabolism or burn-off as they relate to alcohol ingestion. It is true that the alcohol percentage in Mr. Fletcher's body does not tell us when he drank the alcohol. He could have consumed the alcohol sometime shortly before he was admitted to the hospital, or he could have consumed it several hours before. If he had consumed it several hours before, he would have metabolized or burned-off alcohol at a rate somewhere around 0.02 percent per hour. If he had his last drink the night before around midnight, his blood alcohol level could well have been in the neighborhood of 0.30 or higher around 1:00 a.m. It would certainly be possible for someone with a 0.30 blood alcohol level to have greatly impaired judgment, and some people at that level are capable of harboring violent thoughts. And, if he was interviewed later when he was sober, it is medically possible that his recollection of activities he engaged in at the 0.30 level would be distorted and inaccurate.

I did conclude that Mr. Fletcher suffered from hepatic cirrhosis, which was evident from the grossly nodular appearance of his liver and, on microscopic exam, the prominent chronic inflammation of his portal tracts and the fibrous bands. I am aware that when he was hospitalized, the diagnosis included findings of alcohol abuse, copious drinking, that he was severely intoxicated when admitted, that he had to be detoxified before release from the hospital, and that he had a history of alcoholism. Chronic alcoholics with cirrhosis of the liver can suffer from atrophy of the brain, they can have impaired clotting of the blood, and they can be at higher risk for the development of subdural hemorrhages.

It is true that I don't know what activities Mr. Fletcher was engaged in following his release from the hospital, and I cannot say with medical certainty that he did not fall and injure himself in some way on the day he was found dead. But I can say that the injuries I observed in my autopsy examination led me to conclude with a reasonable degree of medical certainty that Mr. Fletcher died as a result of a subdural hemorrhage consistent with infliction on November 7, YR-2.

As to the recent healing fractures of the fourth and fifth lateral ribs, I am not saying that they were the product of the same event that produced the fatal head injuries. I described them as mildly displaced healing fractures with a small amount of hemorrhage and callus formation. Those ribs were likely fractured sometime before November 7. I have no history to explain those fractures, so I could not say whether they resulted from a fall, some other accident, or an altercation. I cannot say that whatever caused those injuries did not cause other injuries, but I can say with a reasonable degree of medical certainty that they are of a different origin than the injury that produced the fatal subdural hematoma.

I do know of Dr. Leslie Sewell. I am aware that Dr. Sewell has made telephone inquiries at our office about this case, and I understand from the District Attorney's Office that Dr. Sewell has expressed the opinion that there is insufficient evidence to determine whether the subdural hemorrhage occurred prior to the altercation of November 7, and that Dr. Sewell also suggested that the cause of death was solely Mr. Fletcher's chronic alcoholism and cirrhosis. I am aware that Dr. Sewell is of the opinion also that the injuries causing the fractured ribs could have initiated the process that resulted in the fatal subdural hemorrhage. As I expressed just moments ago, I not only do not share that opinion, I am medically certain that the opinion is erroneous. The decedent, Mr. Fletcher, had blunt force trauma to his face and blunt trauma inside his head that cannot be discounted. I know that Dr. Sewell was a professional associate in the Darrow County Medical Examiner's Office for about two years and then took a position with Northern Nita Forensic Pathology Laboratories Marshall City. While Dr. Sewell and I worked together, we did not always share the same opinions about some of the cases we handled, and we mutually agreed that Dr. Sewell was probably better off practicing privately.

I hereby certify that the foregoing is a true and correct transcription of the testimony of Dr. Lou Tost on July 20, YR-1, at the preliminary hearing in *State v. Bloodworth*, in the Darrow County Municipal Court, Nita City, Nita.

Certified by:

Culley Rikard

CULLEY RIKARD
Court Reporter

TESTIMONY OF BILLY HERMAN AT PRELIMINARY HEARING[3]

Direct Examination

I own a used car dealership in Nita City. I live at the Riverfront Plaza condominium at number 408. I have lived there for over three years. I am single, but I am engaged to be married. I was acquainted with Ken Fletcher. He was a neighbor. I would see him around the complex, and on occasion I would talk with him, and once in a while would have a beer with him. I was aware that he had a drinking problem, and I also wondered if he had a drug problem as well, but I never saw him take any drugs. When he was drunk, he wasn't an ugly drunk. When I saw him drinking I would describe his behavior as mellow, sometimes a little confused, and on occasion I saw him stagger. But I never saw him violent, and I never heard him threaten anyone, and I certainly never saw him hurt or threaten to hurt anyone. I never saw him possess a knife or ever use or display a knife. That was not the Ken Fletcher I knew.

I became aware that he was injured and taken to the hospital in early November YR-2. I never witnessed any event where he was injured, but there certainly was a lot of talk around Riverfront Plaza about the incident that led to his being hospitalized. Leading up to the time of his injury, he did seem like he was drunk a lot. To the best of my recollection, I believe I saw him drunk within twenty-four hours of when he was taken to the hospital. I knew that his wife left him and when the real estate market with south, he really had a double whammy.

I knew Mr. Bloodworth, the defendant. He lived in the complex too. And I remember I saw both Ken and Mr. Bloodworth together on at least two occasions. They certainly appeared to know each other. One time, I saw the two talking. Ken appeared wobbly, probably drunk, and Mr. Bloodworth looked pretty angry. I heard him say something like, "Don't try that again with me." I couldn't tell you what it was about, but I do know that on another occasion, before this happened, I saw the two together in the Riverfront Plaza elevator, and it looked to me like the defendant bought a watch from Ken. Then Ken got off the elevator, and he told me he didn't want to ride in the elevator with Mr. Bloodworth anymore. I found that curious, since they apparently had a conversation about the watch. I could not tell you an exact date for either of these events, but they were both within two weeks of the time he was injured, and the elevator incident took place first.

When you ask me if I ever heard the defendant accuse Ken of taking his billfold, I am sure I didn't hear that or I would remember that.

I remember about ten days before Ken's hospitalization that I heard Mr. Bloodworth talking on a cell phone. I don't know who he was talking to, but I remember that he said, "If you mess with my stuff, I'll mess you up."

---

[3] The transcript of Billy Herman's testimony was excerpted so that only Billy Herman's answers are reprinted here. Assume that this is a true and accurate rendering of Billy Herman's answers. The testimony was given at the preliminary hearing on July 20, YR-1, in the Darrow County Municipal Court, Nita City, Nita.

Cross-Examination

In the three years that I lived at the complex, I only saw Ken and Mr. Bloodworth together two times. As I said earlier, the first was at a Plaza outdoor party. There were a lot of the residents there. I heard a few words exchanged between the two of them. After that, I did not see them together again that night. I didn't see them drinking together, or laughing, or sitting together. Then I saw them in the Plaza elevator. I never saw them in each other's condos or in a car together.

I didn't report any of these incidents to the police or to the Riverfront Plaza Security Office, and I did not make any notes of any of the incidents I have testified to. I didn't see any reason to. But when you ask me if I can be certain they happened, yes, I can. I just could not tell you the exact date or who else might have witnessed these incidents.

It is true that I opened my door one time when Ken had his hand on the doorknob. I wouldn't call it wiggling the doorknob, but he did have his hand on it. It was in the daytime. Now that you have refreshed my recollection by showing me the statement I gave Detective Howard on November 14, YR-2, I guess I did tell Detective Howard that it took place at 9:30 p.m.

Yes, I did have a run-in with the law several years ago. The State of Nita took my used-car dealer's license away when the Attorney General's Office prosecuted me for falsifying the mileage on several of my cars. I had no knowledge of these incidents. One of my staff must have done it without my knowledge, but I could never get any of my sales or service people to own up to doing it. I pled no contest to the misdemeanor charge. That was about six years ago, but the State restored my license, and I have been continually in business for the last three years. I don't see how that has anything to do with my testifying here. In fact, I resent you even asking me about this. I'm not on trial here.

Redirect Examination

When I saw Ken with his hand on the doorknob, I said, "What the hell are you doing here?" I was going to call security, but I didn't, because he said, "I must be at the wrong condo," or "I guess I got the wrong condo." And he apologized for the mistake. He then staggered away.

I hereby certify that the foregoing is a true and correct transcription of the testimony of Billy Herman on July 20, YR-1, at the preliminary hearing in *State v. Bloodworth*, in the Darrow County Municipal Court, Nita City, Nita.

Certified by:

Culley Rikard

CULLEY RIKARD
Court Reporter

TESTIMONY OF KERRY WESTLAKE AT PRELIMINARY HEARING[4]

Direct Examination

I am the manager of a condominium complex known as Riverfront Plaza, located at 4815 Riverfront Road in Nita City. I have been the manager for the last five years. Prior to that, I was the assistant manager for two years. I reside at the Plaza and have done so for seven years. I feel very fortunate to have that position. Riverfront Plaza is recognized as one of the premier living facilities in Nita City. Part of the Plaza is a home for well-to-do people who want comfortable living accommodations, as well as recreational and fitness opportunities. While most residents pay a membership fee along with their rental fees, some have purchased their accommodations and pay an annual fee to use our other accommodations.

I know Gene Bloodworth, the defendant, and I knew Kenneth Fletcher. I had known Mr. Fletcher for more than two years before he died. Mr. Fletcher moved into condo number 642 on March 14, YR-4, and that was his residence until he died. Mr. Bloodworth, according to our records, moved in January 15, YR-3, but I remember seeing him before that. Both Mr. Fletcher and Mr. Bloodworth paid rental fees.

I have seen the two together on several occasions. As I recall it, even before Mr. Bloodworth moved in, I know I saw them together in Mr. Fletcher's condo. At that time, I didn't know who Mr. Blood-worth was, but it appeared to me that the two certainly knew each other. It appeared that he was visiting Mr. Fletcher on those occasions. I have no idea what they were talking about, and I certainly had no reason to be nosy about it. I saw them at those times when I was making the rounds of the Plaza, and on those multiple times that I saw Mr. Bloodworth in Mr. Fletcher's condo, it was because I either had some reason to contact Mr. Fletcher or his door was open when I was on the sixth floor. Then after Mr. Bloodworth moved in January to the fifth floor, I remember seeing Mr. Fletcher in Mr. Bloodworth's condo for sure on one occasion and maybe more. Again, I don't know what they were talking about, but it was apparent they knew each other and had some reason to meet together. I had no reason to be suspicious then, but I do now. I mean by that, in view of what happened last November 7, there was some very serious problem between the two of them.

I didn't see what happened on November 7. In fact, I wasn't even informed about that until some-time in the morning when someone, I don't recall who, told me the cops had been there early in the morning, and Mr. Fletcher was taken on a stretcher to the hospital, and he was in really bad condi-tion. I tried to find out what happened, and all I heard was something about a bunch of pills on the floor and there was a horrible fight. In thinking back, I remembered Mr. Bloodworth talking to me about four days before November 7. He said that someone "ripped off my billfold that had several hundred dollars, and I'm gonna find out who did it." I asked him whether he thought it was a burglar and whether his room was locked. He said, "Yeah, sure, I always lock my room." I couldn't under-stand that. We have very upscale and secure door locks. They are designed to be virtually burglar proof. The tumblers are protected in a thick steel case. I am not an expert, and I can't tell you why,

---

[4] The transcript of Kerry Westlake's testimony was excerpted so that only Kerry Westlake's answers are reprinted here. Assume that this is a true and accurate rendering of Kerry Westlake's answers. The testimony was given at the preliminary hearing on July 20, YR-1, in the Darrow County Municipal Court, Nita City, Nita.

but that is what we learned before we purchased them. I do remember Mr. Bloodworth saying, "I don't have proof yet, but I'm going to get it. And when I do, the person that did this is going to be sorry." I can tell you that I have never given a key to Mr. Bloodworth's condo to Mr. Fletcher, and we are not missing any of the keys to that unit.

I have no reason to want to testify against Mr. Bloodworth. In fact, on occasion Mr. Bloodworth and I have engaged in small talk or chatter. I remember that when I first knew that he was a former big league ballplayer for the Pirates, I was pretty interested. I played ball in college and later a little semi-pro ball, and I would have given my right arm, well, not really, but I wanted to play pro ball. So, I was fascinated. I learned that he still worked occasionally as a scout, and he was active in the community in bringing a triple-A ball team to Nita City and building a modern ball park.

He felt that the reason he never was hired as a coach or a commentator was because MLB knew about his manslaughter conviction. He said, "That ruined my career. Those bastard Philly cops railroaded me. It was a classic case of self-defense, and I ended up doing jail time and lost my career." He was pretty upset. I remember this because he got into the details of the manslaughter. What he said was that two guys, I think he said Phillies fans, were really upset that he was a Pirate. He said that the Phillies and the Pirate fans all hate each other because they come from the same state, and they have a pretty big rivalry. Anyway, he said these two guys started calling the Pirates a bunch of pansies, and then they came at him and a couple of his friends and started a fight, and he and his friends defended themselves. He hit this one guy who fell back and hit his head on a bar rail, and the guy died, apparently from a hemorrhage. He said the cops believed some of the Phillies fans who claimed that he sucker punched the guy without warning, and that is apparently what the jury believed. He said the jurors were as dumb as the cops.

I certainly didn't want to rile up Mr. Bloodworth. He seemed pretty angry thinking about it, but after a while he calmed down, and I told him that I really admired what he had achieved in his career, and I told him that I still had my old glove and a ball, and asked if he would autograph the ball. We then went to my unit, I got out the ball, and he wrote, "To Kerry, a true Pirates fan," and he signed it. I thought that was pretty nice of him.

The only knowledge I have about possible drug use by Mr. Bloodworth is what I heard about the pills that were found, and what Mr. Bloodworth once told me. He said that his girlfriend needed to tone down her drug use. I have no idea who his girlfriend is.

As to Mr. Fletcher's use of alcohol or drugs, I can certainly say that I have seen him pretty seriously inebriated on multiple occasions. He had the reputation of being a heavy drinker, and apparently he got worse after his business began to fail and his wife left him. I would see him stagger in sometimes late at night, and I can remember occasions when he had difficulty finding his own condo. I do remember one time when I had to lead him to his place on the sixth floor. That must have been sometime around July or August of that year. I do remember Mr. Fletcher telling me that someone got very mad at him when he mistook their condo for his, but he didn't give any details. I can tell you that it couldn't have been a very big problem, because my office never received any complaints about this kind of conduct. I never saw him act violently, and I never saw him with any kind of weapon including a knife.

The last time I saw Mr. Fletcher was sometime around 10:30 in the morning on the day of his death. Somebody mentioned that he was lying directly outside his door on the sixth floor, and two or three people were checking him, including one of the cleaning ladies. I went directly up and saw that he was lying unconscious, and we called 911. Within five to ten minutes, two emergency types showed up and took charge. After about five minutes of what looked like resuscitation efforts, they said he was dead and had apparently been dead for a while. Later, people apparently from the morgue took his body away. Apparently, no one ever saw him fall down or saw how he came to be lying on the floor.

Sometime after Mr. Fletcher's death, I was contacted by Detective Howard and asked whether I had a Facebook account on my computer and I told Detective Howard I did. I explained that it was important that key employees at the Plaza be available and helpful to our residents, so I maintained a private account but the Plaza informed all of our residents that they were all listed as friends, and it was common that many residents listed me as a friend. Many of those residents, including Mr. Fletcher, Mr. Herman, and Mr. Bloodworth, sent me Facebook messages on a regular basis. Detective Howard asked if I would permit Detective Howard to review the Facebook pages of those three residents, and I agreed and found three pages, Exhibits 10, 11, and 14. I showed them to Detective Howard and made copies of them for Detective Howard, who thanked me and took the copies.

Cross-Examination

It's true that as the manager of Riverfront Plaza I am responsible for selecting residents and for making sure that there are no security problems. That's why we retain security officers to check the premises and why we run background checks on potential employees or clients. I did feel chagrined and embarrassed that I did not know of this incident until much later on the morning of November 7. I have discussed that incident with our owners and have spoken with an attorney for the corporation about potential liability for this incident. I refuse to answer your question about what I said to our lawyer and what our lawyer said to me. I was told that our conversations are protected by the attorney-client relationship. (Objection by defense counsel and request to require witness to answer was denied by the court.) When I spoke with Detective Howard back in November YR-2, I did tell the detective that in hindsight we probably made a mistake in accepting Mr. Bloodworth's application. No, I am sure I didn't ask the detective to keep that quiet, and I don't remember discussing a civil suit with the detective. I don't remember telling the detective about the times I saw the two together in their condos only after discussing a civil suit. As I said, I don't think we even discussed a civil suit, but if I did, the timing of my discussing seeing the two together in the condos had nothing to do with that.

I have never seen Mr. Bloodworth in possession of a knife. I have not heard him threaten anyone other than what he said about his billfold being stolen. I have never heard him say anything about Mr. Fletcher, and I have not seen him with Mr. Fletcher when Mr. Bloodworth seemed angry.

I do remember hearing residents of the Plaza occasionally discuss Mr. Fletcher and his drinking. It happened more than once that I heard them say that he was an "alky," that sometimes he reeked of alcohol, and that on some occasions he had made a fool of himself. I would agree that at the Plaza he had the reputation of being a drunk. And, as I said before, I do remember hearing him talk about someone being mad at him because of a mistake he made in going to their condo, but I can't tell you whether they said he was turning a doorknob at a condo or not.

Yes, I'm glad that Mr. Bloodworth is no longer at the Plaza, and it is true that I would not want him to return. Right after his arrest, he left the Plaza and we cleaned out his condo and then found another very nice married couple that now lives there.

I hereby certify that the foregoing is a true and correct transcription of the testimony of Kerry Westlake on July 20, YR-1, at the preliminary hearing in *State v. Bloodworth*, in the Darrow County Municipal Court, Nita City, Nita.

Certified by:

Culley Rikard

CULLEY RIKARD
Court Reporter

STATEMENTS OF DEFENSE WITNESSES

STATEMENT OF CHRIS SINGLETON[1]

I live at the Riverfront Plaza Condominium in Nita City, and have lived there for about four-and-a-half or five years. I know both Gene Bloodworth and Kenneth Fletcher. Gene Bloodworth, I call him "Guts. That's right, "Guts Bloodworth." That's what they used to call him when he played for the Pirates. That was because he always tried harder than anyone else on the team. He was always the first one to take batting practice and the last one to leave the ballpark. He was known for doing whatever it took to get something done, whether it was crashing against the fence to catch a fly ball or sliding spikes up to break up a double play. And he wouldn't let anyone push him around. I recall a pitcher for the Phillies threw inside head-high after Guts had hit a home run on his last at bat. They had to pull Guts off the pitcher, and they were both thrown out of the game. On TV afterward, Guts was asked about it and he said something like, "There are rules in baseball that you don't break, and if you do, there's always a response."

I know all this because for a while I ran the concession stand where the Pirates sold jerseys, caps, autographed baseballs, and stuff like that at PNC Park for about three years. I knew Guts then, and after I left Pittsburg and moved to Nita City I read about his retirement. I couldn't believe it when I read that he was convicted of manslaughter. It ruined his career. I wrote him when he did joint time and suggested that he move out of Pittsburg and consider living in Nita City. To my surprise, I got an answer. He said he would consider it. He was disgusted with Pittsburg, and felt the cops, the prosecutors, and the community let him down. I told him about the Plaza, and when he was released he came to Nita City and contacted me. I put him in touch with the Plaza office, and whamo, he moved in.

We have been close friends since. I have a memorabilia and sports store on Front Street in Nita City known as Best Sports Stuff, and Guts has been good enough to sign autographs and merchandise, and he sometimes comes down and helps me when I'm short staffed. In spite of his conviction, he has been well received in Nita City because he has made an effort in our community to help youngsters in sports, especially baseball. As a result, the Nita City Lions Club honored Guts for his community work in YR-3.

Guts was surprised that Nita City's baseball team was only B league and had an old, small stadium, and when I told him that I had made efforts through several channels including the Chamber of Commerce and the City Council to build an AAA team for Nita City, he suggested that the two of us could offer being a significant part of the team ownership if the city would help fund a modern stadium. In my years both in Pittsburgh and Nita City, I had done well in my business and Guts told me that in his last five years with the Pirates he had banked and invested millions, and ownership of the team would put him back in baseball in a positive way in his new home. For the last two years, Guts and I, along with community leaders, have made progress and but for these charges, I believe we would have had a triple A team set for next year. Of course, now Guts has been cut off the community efforts, and this is a crying shame, for he would have been a perfect leader of the effort.

I remember Ken Fletcher. I think most people at the Plaza would remember him. He had the reputation of being a wasted drunk. I guess he had some success in his life, because I heard that in the '90s and the early twenty-first century he was a very successful realtor. I understand he specialized

---

[1] This statement was given to defense investigator Frank Gustine in his office on December 14, YR-2.

in high-end stuff, both residential and commercial. When the economy hit the skids, he went down in a big way. People said that he always had a golden spoon and inherited the realty firm from his father, and when things got bad, he didn't know what to do, so he turned to alcohol. I remember him telling me about this big estate he owned in the Garden District, and after the bad times came along, his wife got pretty angry at his drinking and she divorced him. She got the house, he kept the business, and then he pretty much crashed. He told me there were some lawsuits and he was running low on money because he had to hire a lawyer to take care of the newest suit. He did brag that he was well-off, but it looked to me that he was going to have to supplement his income somehow. Like a lot of people, one part of him I sort of liked, but the other part was both pathetic and a turn-off. He would get so drunk that he didn't even know how to find his way back to his condo on the sixth floor.

You ask whether I ever saw Fletcher with a knife. As I recall it, I remember seeing him once or twice with a funny knife. I think it was a folding knife. I couldn't tell you what it looked like exactly, and I can't tell you the exact occasion, but my best recollection is when he was near the condo garage and he was cleaning his fingernails. I thought it was sort of a strange way to do that. It was some time ago, at least a year ago, that I saw that. I have never seen Guts with any kind of knife, other than when I have seen him eating. So far as I know, Guts doesn't even own a knife.

I can tell you that in the years that I have known and see Guts and Fletcher, I have never seen them together in the same condo. I understand that someone said the two have been seen together dating back to before Guts moved in. Well, I have been living at the Plaza, as I said, for close to five years, and I haven't seen the two together at any time, much less in their respective condos. And I have never heard talk from anyone else that the two had meetings or were close in any way. My impression from knowing both is that Guts would not have much to do with Fletcher. Besides, I know that Guts's girlfriend, Sadie McLish, was pretty important to Guts, and he spent most of his time with her. I used to see the two of them in and around his condo. I think Guts and Sadie were going to get married, but this whole thing put that on the back burner. I think you know who I would believe between Guts and Fletcher. I have never known Guts to lie about anything. He is a straight shooter all the way.

I heard a lot about the fight between Guts and Fletcher. I wasn't there and didn't see anything, but Guts called me, woke me up sometime after midnight, must have been around 1:30 or 2:00 in the morning. And he told me what just happened. He told me this guy broke into Guts's condo and tried to get some money and tried to kill him with a knife. He thought the guy was the drunk. I later learned he was talking about Fletcher. I don't think he mentioned his name when he called. He said he thought the guy thought Guts had some big time money. He was in bed around midnight when he woke up and the guy was standing over him in his bedroom. The guy yelled at him, "I want your money." Guts yelled at him, jumped out of bed, and tried to protect himself, swinging at the guy. Guts told me it was so dark he couldn't tell who it was. He said they battled into the living room, and he hit the guy and knocked him down. Guts said when the guy fell down for the first time he saw the knife. He described it as kind of silver, and it fell on the floor. He said he found pills on the floor. He asked me, "What should I do?" I told him to call the cops, and he said he would. He called the cops. I didn't go up to his condo.

Later that morning, he told me that after he knocked out Fletcher, he then tried to clean up the room by picking up some of the pills. He said they were prescription pills, I think he said either pain pills or sleeping pills. He also told me that he thinks Fletcher was looking for drugs, because Fletcher apparently spilled some drugs from their bottles when he broke into Guts's condo. As I understand it from Guts, he had in the past bought a drink for Fletcher a time or two, and had pulled out a one-hundred dollar bill on one occasion, and Fletcher commented that Guts must be doing okay. Guts told him that as a ballplayer he always carried several hundred dollars in his wallet. Of course, having known Guts for quite a while, I know that Guts was very well off. Poor people don't own a car like Guts's Porsche Boxster S. Guts told me he thinks that Fletcher got drunk and then decided to get money by stealing Guts's wallet. Anyway, the cops came and took Fletcher to the hospital. Guts told me he had to clean blood off the floor.

I think the next day Guts said he heard that the hospital confirmed Fletcher was really drunk, but as soon as they could sober him up, they were going to release him, as his injuries were minor. Guts said that he was going to press charges because it was scary to think someone could break into your home in the middle of the night and attack you. I told Guts I agreed, and it was pretty obvious Fletcher had gone out of his mind. I know that people who are not aggressive when they are drinking can sometimes do violent and stupid things. My uncle used to act that way when he got drunk. One time he got home around 2:00 in the morning, went to the garage and got a pickaxe, and went over to the home of the Presbyterian minister and yelled at him to come out and fight him. Fortunately for him, the minister wouldn't press charges, and my uncle finally decided to quit drinking.

I have been asked if there is anything in my past that might affect my credibility as a witness. I think I can honestly say that there is not. Sometimes in life, people can be falsely accused. It sounds to me like that is what's happening here to Guts. I was put through that shortly after I moved to Nita City and opened my sports memorabilia store on Front Street. Among other merchandise, we sold autographed baseballs. We sold them from MLB teams. These were not baseballs that were endorsed by major league baseball, but there was no law against selling them. We relied on sources in several major league cities, and we were assured by them that the signatures were genuine. We received a shipment from Cincinnati with signatures from the Reds. We sold them as authentic in reliance on our sources. As it turned out, most were not authentic. The problem was that we could not produce any witnesses to establish how we relied on the company, called *REDSWARE*.

It turned out to be a phony, and all the names of the staff were falsified. So I was prosecuted by the Darrow County DA's Office Consumer Fraud Division. I agreed to pay a civil judgment to Darrow County, to the State of Nita, and to about fourteen victims who bought the baseballs from my store. So in total I was out lawyer fees, about ten thousand dollars in fines, a restitution order to reimburse the victims to the tune of about two thousand dollars. I also pled no contest to a misdemeanor crime of theft by false pretenses. They put me on probation, and one of the conditions of probation was that if there was any evidence of my handling any products that were not authentic, I would have my probation violated and I would serve a year of county jail. That was about four years ago, and I since have been approved by the Better Business Bureau of Nita City. I am a member of the Lions Club, my business has been very successful, and I guess you could say that I learned from that experience that whatever the cause, I am responsible for anything that happens in my business.

I have read the above statement consisting of three pages, and it is true and correct.

Signed:

Chris Singleton
_____
Chris Singleton

Dec. 14, YR-2
_____
Date

Witnessed:

Frank Gustine
_____
Frank Gustine

12/14/YR-2
_____
Date:

STATEMENT OF SADIE McLISH[2]

I have known Gene Bloodworth for about three years. You might say we're engaged. We expected to get married sometime around Christmas of this year, but his arrest for murder took care of that. I have been a part-time actress, doing some local drama productions, and I have appeared in a few supporting roles in television productions. I have also written two books. The first, *Get Back Up*, was a written semi-documentary of my twenties disguised with fictional characters. It dealt with some of my successes and some of my, you might say, shortcomings. The second, *Step Ladder*, was more of a how-to-do-it book for young women, particularly those young women who come from a broken home and have to make it on their own. When I was in my early twenties, I was inspired by a show on *Oprah*, where these young women told their stories about how they turned their lives around by sheer determination. Most had gone on to college or some kind of educational program. That motivated me to move away from my friends, get a straight job, and go to Nita Community College at nights, and then on to Nita State College for my degree. I felt that my story might help others, and so I wrote both of these books. While neither book was a bestseller, the proceeds have helped me enormously over the last seven years.

I met Gene at a function downtown where Nita City was trying to put together a business package that would attract a triple-A baseball club. I was working with a firm that put together video presentations for business purposes. I was doing a narrative and Gene was being interviewed for a segment. Something clicked the moment we met. I liked and admired his strength and confidence, and I certainly thought he was a handsome man. It didn't hurt my confidence any when he told me that I was one of the most attractive and interesting women he had ever met. We started dating, and although we had separate residences, sometimes we spent time in the Plaza, where he had a beautiful condo, and sometimes we spent time in Lake Grounds in Nita City, where I have a place. It didn't hurt that I followed baseball and even remember when he played for the Pirates. I think you could say that I know Gene as well as anyone and better than most. He is a gentleman. He has always treated me with the greatest respect. I cannot believe that anyone would think Gene would do anything wrong. It blows my mind that the authorities in Philadelphia ever prosecuted him for defending himself, and now it is unthinkable that history repeats itself here in Nita City.

Besides just vouching for Gene's credibility, I can add several things that I know with certainty. Gene does not own any kind of knife, and never has since I met him. I have never heard him discuss the subject of using a knife. I know that Gene had no relationship of any kind with Kenneth Fletcher. He looked on Mr. Fletcher like most people did. Fletcher, unfortunately, had the reputation of being a severe alcoholic, a pathetic, broken man who could not pull himself up to recover from bad things that had happened to him. In many ways, he was pretty similar to my father, who became an alcoholic, mistreated my mother and my sister and two brothers, and who finally left the family. That's just one reason why I had to make it on my own as I grew up. Anyway, I can tell you that Gene did not meet with Fletcher, didn't have any business contact with him, and generally had no contact with him. On occasion, Gene would say something about Mr. Fletcher, but it usually was something like how he had made a fool of himself drinking at the bar, or how he fell down and hurt himself, or how he annoyed people near the pool.

---

[2] This statement was given to defense investigator Frank Gustine in his office on December 14, YR-2.

I was not at Gene's place on November 6 or 7. I had spent a couple of days there on, I believe, November 4 and 5, and I still had some of my things at his place. I may have left some of my medication, since I have to take some of it every day. Because of what I have been through in my life, I have been prescribed medication for anxiety and stress, both Xanax and Valium. I don't take them daily, but on occasions when I feel stress, I do take one or the other. Also, occasionally I have to take pain medication, and so when that happens, I take Vicodin. So that I don't have to transport these pills, I keep a supply at Gene's place. I understand that on November 7, Mr. Fletcher got drunk and tried to rob Gene when he was sleeping, and apparently wanted both money and drugs. Somehow, he found some of my pills, which I had left there. They would have been in the bathroom cabinet. So far as I know, Gene doesn't take any medication except some anti-inflammatory stuff for some old sports injuries, particularly his shoulder. Gene told me that pills had been spilled on the floor and he cleaned them up and threw them away. I don't know if that happened before the police arrived or after. I certainly wasn't going to take any dirty pills if he had saved them. I told him that was fine.

While I wasn't there when this happened, I can certainly say that Gene would not have invited Mr. Fletcher into his condo, and certainly would not have invited several people to his place on the evening of November 6 and early morning of November 7. We were planning on meeting early on November 7, and Gene always wants to get his sleep. He told me once that sleep was always a premium when he was playing professional baseball, and since he retired, he religiously went to bed early.

In response to your questions about my background, as I told you, in my early years I had a tough time. After I ran away from home, I lived for a short time on the street, and then found some friends who had similar backgrounds. Several of those friends in my late teens took drugs on a regular basis. There was weed, crank, speed, and even hallucinogenic mushrooms. I fooled around with some of this stuff and got busted. I knew it was illegal, and I knew it wasn't good for me, but I was young and stupid and they were my only friends. I was able to pull myself up by my bootstraps and get out of this, but my legacy from my misspent youth was an occasional lapse with drugs.

Instead of taking illegal drugs, I was now able to get prescriptions. But when I took some of these, especially when I took more than one at a time, it had a powerful effect on me, and so there were two occasions when I was charged with a crime. The first was a DUI, that is, under the influence of alcohol and drugs. That was about two years ago. I was by myself coming back from a date with Gene. The second was embarrassing. I was on a job, putting on a production for the Chamber of Commerce at a meeting of the Nita City Council. I had been working on this for several days with little sleep and was stressed, and decided to take a Valium. Then the guy in charge of this effort asked me to join him at the bar for a glass of wine before we went to City Hall. By the time I got to City Hall, I didn't even know where I was, much less what to do. Someone apparently called the cops, and I was arrested for drunk in public. It was terrible. I was placed in a drunk tank at the county jail, and the guy in charge bailed me out. I ended up pleading guilty and got the standard sentence of forty days in the county jail, suspended, placed on what they called summary probation for a year. The Chamber of Commerce wasn't very happy, and I wasn't asked to do any more work for them or for the company that put it together. Recently, Gene and I have had several discussions about my medication, and I agreed that I would cut back, and I have.

I have read the above statement consisting of two pages, and it is true and correct.

Signed:

Sadie McLish
Sadie McLish

December 14, YR-2
Date

Witnessed:

Frank Gustine
Frank Gustine

12/14/YR-2
Date:

Correspondence from Dr. Leslie Sewell

NORTHERN NITA FORENSIC PATHOLOGY LABORATORIES

St. Luke's Medical Building, Suite 410
1601 Heffernan Drive
Marshall City, Nita 85424
(721) 555-6066

March 18, YR-1

Sharon Nagy, Esq.
Nagy Bahr & Behrman
868 Stock Drive
Nita City, Nita 85522

Dear Ms. Nagy:

Thank you for your referral of Mr. Bloodworth's case. As you requested, I have reviewed the case materials which you submitted and I have enclosed a copy of my curriculum vitae. Those materials are the police reports prepared by Detective Howard and Joan Russell; an autopsy report prepared by Dr. Lou Tost; the medical records of the Darrow County Medical Center concerning the treatment of Kenneth Fletcher; and copies of the photos and diagrams.

At autopsy, Kenneth Fletcher was confirmed to be suffering from cirrhosis of the liver due to chronic alcoholism. Mr. Fletcher had been involved in an altercation on November 7, YR-2, and was admitted to the Darrow County Medical Center, where he was found to be suffering from a left-sided subdural hematoma, which was not clinically significant, and was stable. Mr. Fletcher's blood alcohol level upon admission to the hospital was 0.2165. Mr. Fletcher was evaluated by specialized physicians at the hospital and was judged to be stable. He was discharged on November 10, YR-2, without any treatment for his subdural hemorrhage. He was expected to recover completely and was not expected to die from his subdural hemorrhage.

Mr. Fletcher was found lying unresponsive in front of his condo three days later on November 13, YR-2. Autopsy revealed acute blunt force trauma of the head, acute and chronic subdural hemorrhages with acute congestive brain swelling, and brain herniation.

Mr. Fletcher was a chronic alcoholic who suffered from cirrhosis of the liver. Chronic alcoholics with cirrhosis of the liver suffer from atrophy of the brain and impaired clotting of the blood; they are very prone to subdural hemorrhages even with the slightest amounts of acceleration-deceleration forces. Chronic alcoholics are also known to suffer from toxic injury to the regions of the brain that are responsible for balance; they are known to be very prone to ataxia, frequent falls, and traumatic brain injuries. At autopsy, Mr. Fletcher was confirmed to have suffered both acute and chronic subdural hemorrhages, accompanied by old healing fractures of the lateral fourth to sixth ribs. He also exhibited evidence of acute brain injury, which began after he had been discharged from the hospital.

There is insufficient forensic pathologic and medical evidence to determine with a reasonable degree of medical certainty that Mr. Fletcher did not sustain subdural hemorrhage prior to his altercation on November 7, YR-2. There is also insufficient evidence to reasonably exculpate falls and further traumatic brain injuries sustained by Mr. Fletcher after he was discharged from the hospital. In fact, autopsy revealed acute traumatic brain injuries, which had occurred after he was discharged from the hospital.

It is pertinent to note that a variety of doctors who attended Mr. Fletcher evaluated him and judged him to be stable before he was discharged home. Mr. Fletcher's injuries lacked reasonable lethal capacity and were not expected to kill him. Being a chronic alcoholic with a documented blood alcohol level of 0.216 percent upon hospital admission, there is an overwhelming medical probability that he sustained traumatic brain injuries before his altercation and after his altercation. Alcohol is a brain toxin, which accentuates the lethal capacity of even the mildest forms of brain injury that should not kill an individual who is not intoxicated by alcohol.

In summary, therefore, it is my opinion that, with a reasonable degree of medical certainty, Kenneth Fletcher died as a result of complications of chronic alcoholism and cirrhosis of the liver. Chronic alcoholism and the deleterious outcomes of chronic alcoholism precipitated traumatic brain injuries and accentuated the lethal capacity of his traumatic brain injuries, which would not have resulted in his death if he was not a chronic alcoholic with permanent brain and liver damage. There is a significant degree of medical certainty that Kenneth Fletcher would still have died without his physical altercation on November YR-2. More likely than not, he may have been involved in another physical altercation after he was discharged from the hospital, or he may have suffered numerous falls after he was discharged from the hospital. Both physical altercations and falls after his discharge from the hospital could have independently precipitated his sudden death. Autopsy failed to identify the syndrome of repetitive traumatic brain injury in this case.

ADDITIONAL BACKGROUND INFORMATION

There are a few areas that need amplification. I have examined hundreds of bodies at death scenes of all kinds, as well as a number of homicide scenes after the body was transported. I have performed over 1,500 medico-legal autopsies and have supervised another seventy-five to one hundred. At least 20 percent of those cases involved head wounds. I have qualified and testified as an expert witness in the States of Nita and California and in federal courts over seventy times. I have appeared in criminal proceedings for both the prosecution and defense, and have been retained by plaintiff's and defense attorneys in civil matters. The areas of my testimony have included cause of death, natural disease, and the nature and causation of various injuries present in both deceased and surviving persons, including head wounds. I have rendered an expert opinion in court concerning head wounds in approximately fifteen to twenty cases. I have also been involved in interpreting results of serology and toxicology testing. Northern Nita Forensic Pathology Laboratories provides forensic pathology services for Marshall County. I currently perform thirty to forty autopsies per month. Additionally, I have consulted for private attorneys, public defenders, and district attorneys in several dozen cases.

If I testify as an expert in this case, you should know that Dr. Lou Tost and I once worked together in the Darrow County Medical Examiner's Office. When Dr. Tost was appointed Medical Director of that office, I chose to leave and come to Marshall City with Northern Nita Forensic Pathology Laboratories. While I respect Dr. Tost's medical qualifications and ability, I found it difficult, as did a number of other medical associates, to work with Dr. Tost. Since then I have testified on several occasions in opposition to the conclusions of Dr. Tost.

To date, I have devoted eight hours in case review, analysis, and the preparation of this report at the standard rate of $350 per hour, for a total of $2,800. Professional time devoted to preparing for and attending court will be billed at the same rate. In the event that you need a copy of my professional CV, I will provide an up-to-date copy. If you require additional information or would like to discuss the case further, please feel free to call me.

Sincerely,

Leslie Sewell

Leslie Sewell, MD, MBA

NORTHERN NITA FORENSIC PATHOLOGY LABORATORIES

St. Luke's Medical Building, Suite 410
1601 Heffernan Drive
Marshall City, Nita 85424
(721) 555-6066

January 15, YR-0

Sharon Nagy, Esq.
Nagy Bahr & Behrman
868 Stock Drive
Nita City, Nita 85522

      Re: *State v. Bloodworth*

Dear Ms. Nagy:

I received your subpoena to appear and testify in the case of *State v. Bloodworth*. As I mentioned previously, it will be necessary for me to further review my records and perform further research on the issues presented. Professional time devoted to preparing for and attending court will be billed at the rate of $350 per hour, and my travel time from Marshall City will be included in the resulting fee. I am attaching an up-to-date copy of my professional CV.

If you require additional information or would like to discuss the case further, please feel free to call me.

Sincerely,

Leslie Sewell
Leslie Sewell, MD, MBA

Att:

LESLIE SEWELL, M.D.

1601 Heffernan Drive, Suite 410
Marshall City, Nita 85424
(721) 555-6066
(721) 555-6067 (Fax)
lsewell@nnfpl.nita (EMail)

EDUCATIONAL BACKGROUND

BS, with great distinction in Biology and Chemistry, University of Pittsburgh, YR-20
MD, Medical University of South Carolina, YR-16
Internship in Pathology, College of Physicians & Surgeons of Columbia University, YR-15
Residency in Anatomical and Clinical Pathology, University of California–Davis, YR-14 to YR-11
Fellowship training in Forensic Pathology, San Diego Coroner's Office, University of California–Davis, YR-11 to YR-10
MBA, Graziadio School of Business, Pepperdine University, YR-4

EMPLOYMENT HISTORY

Forensic Pathologist, San Diego Coroner's Office, YR-10 to YR-7
Forensic Pathologist, Darrow County Medical Examiner's Office, YR -7 to YR-5
Forensic Pathologist, Northern Nita Forensic Pathology Laboratories, YR-4 to present

CERTIFICATION AND LICENSURE

California Physician's and Surgeon's License—July YR-14
Nita Physician's and Surgeon's License—YR-7
American Board of Pathology—Anatomic Pathology—July YR-9
American Board of Pathology—Clinical Pathology—July YR-8
American Board of Pathology—Forensic Pathology—November YR-7
American Board of Forensic Examiners—September YR-4

PROFESSIONAL ASSOCIATIONS

Fellow, College of American Pathologists, YR-10 to present
Member, National Association of Medical Examiners, YR-9 to present
Member, American Academy of Forensic Sciences, YR-7 to present
Member, American Medical Association, YR-11 to present
Member, Nita Medical Society, YR-7 to present

TEACHING EXPERIENCE

Assistant and Associate Professor of Pathology, Nita University, YR-6 to present.
Guest lecturer, University of California–Davis, Marshall Community College, Nita State College

PRESENTATIONS

University of California–Davis—"Subdural Hematoma: Disease or Trauma?" May YR-1

Nita State Hospital—Fourth Annual Pathology Forum—"Forensic Aspects of Head Trauma," November YR-3

Marshall County Sheriff-Medical Examiner's Death Investigation Course—"Introduction to Forensic Medicine," August 14, YR-3

PUBLICATIONS

Bonham, M. and Sewell, L., *Determination of Blunt Force Trauma,* Northern Nita Prosecutors Association Monthly Bulletin, June YR-6.

Sewell, L., *Alcoholism as a Death Trigger*, Journal of Forensic Sciences, May YR-4

Salkeld, D. & Sewell, L., *Examination of the Real Evidence in Homicides*, Journal of Nita Criminal Defense Counsel, October YR-1

Sewell, L., *Pathology and Prosecution, the Unholy Alliance*, Journal on Advocacy, February YR-1

CONGRESSIONAL HEARING AND TESTIMONY

Congress of the United States, House of Representatives, Committee on the Judiciary, Field Hearing: Legal Issues Relating to Football Head Injuries, Monday, January 4, YR-2

COMMITTEE APPOINTMENTS

San Diego County Death Review Team, YR-8 to YR-7. Multidisciplinary review team charged with analyzing suspected homicide deaths and recommending investigative and teaching improvements in such cases

Nita SIDS Protocol Committee, Consultant, YR-6 to YR-5. Committee responsible for producing final form of a sudden infant death autopsy protocol for Nita Department of Health, as mandated by Nita SB 1069.

Darrow County Toxicology Review Team, YR-7 to YR-5. Team formed as a pilot program sponsored by the State of Nita to investigate causes and recommend preventive strategies to mortality as a result of toxic substances.

Northern Nita Regional Trauma Quality Improvement Committee, July, YR-4 to present. Acts to review quality assurance for trauma care in Northern Nita counties.

Forensic Sciences Committee, Association of Nita Criminal Defense Counsel, YR-4 to present. Committee establishes standards for forensic experts serving as witnesses in criminal cases.

HONORS, AWARDS AND ACHIEVEMENTS

Co-founder, Brain Injury Research Institute, Nita University, July YR-1

Outstanding Forensic Expert, Nita State Public Defenders' Association, October YR-1

National Delegate, Committee on Interns and Residents, AMA, YR-11

APPENDICES

APPLICABLE NITA CRIMINAL CODE AND VEHICLE CODE SECTIONS

Nita Criminal Code § 100—Murder
Murder is the unlawful killing of a human being or a fetus with malice aforethought.

Nita Criminal Code § 101—First Degree Murder
1. A person commits the crime of first degree murder if, after deliberation and with the intent to cause death of a person other than himself or herself, he or she causes the death of that person or of another person.
2. First degree murder is a felony punishable by confinement in prison for twenty-five years to life.

Nita Criminal Code §102—Second Degree Murder
1. A person commits the crime of second degree murder if:
   a. He or she intentionally, but not after deliberation, causes the death of a person, or
   b. With intent to cause serious bodily injury to a person other than himself or herself, he or she causes the death of that person or of another person
2. Second degree murder is a felony punishable by confinement in prison for fifteen to fifty years.

Nita Criminal Code § 103—Voluntary Manslaughter
1. A person commits the crime of voluntary manslaughter if he or she intentionally, but not after deliberation, causes the death of a person, under circumstances where the act causing the death was performed upon a sudden heat of passion caused by a serious and highly provoking act of the intended victim, affecting the person killing sufficiently to excite an irresistible passion in a reasonable person. However, if between the provocation and the killing there is an interval sufficient for the voice of reason and humanity to be heard, the killing is murder.
2. Voluntary manslaughter is a felony punishable by confinement in prison for seven to twenty years.

Nita Criminal Code § 104—Criminally Negligent Homicide
1. A person commits the crime of criminally negligent homicide, if:
   a. By conduct amounting to criminal negligence, he or she causes the death of a person; or
   b. He or she intentionally causes the death of a person, but believes in good faith that circumstances exist which would justify the killing, but the belief that such circumstances exist is unreasonable.
2. A person acts with criminal negligence when, through a gross deviation from the standard of care that a reasonable person would exercise, he or she fails to perceive a substantial and unjustifiable risk that a result will occur, or that a circumstance exists.
3. Criminally negligent homicide is a misdemeanor punishable by confinement in the county jail for up to one year, or by a fine of up to ten thousand dollars ($10,000), or both.

Nita Criminal Code § 148—Resisting, Delaying, or Obstructing an Officer
1. Every person who willfully resists, delays, or obstructs any peace officer in the discharge or attempt to discharge any duty of his or her office or employment is guilty of a violation of this section.

2. A violation of this section shall be punished by a fine not exceeding one thousand dollars ($1,000), or by imprisonment in a county jail not to exceed one year, or by both that fine and imprisonment.

Nita Criminal Code § 243—Battery on a Police Officer

1. A battery on a peace officer with injury is any willful and unlawful use of force of violence on the person of a peace officer, whether on or off duty, when the peace officer is engaged in the performance of his or her duties, and the person committing the offense knows or reasonably should know that the victim is a peace officer engaged in the performance of his or her duties, and an injury is inflicted on that victim.
2. Battery on a peace officer is punishable by confinement in prison for two to six years or by confinement in the county jail for up to one year.

Nita Criminal Code § 273.5—Spousal Abuse

1. Any person who willfully inflicts upon a person who is his or her spouse, former spouse, cohabitant, former cohabitant, or the mother or father of his or her child, corporal injury resulting in a traumatic condition, is guilty of a felony, and upon conviction thereof shall be punished by imprisonment in the state prison for two, three, or four years, or in a county jail for not more than one year, or by a fine of up to six thousand dollars ($6,000) or by both that fine and imprisonment.

Nita Criminal Code § 415—Disturbing the Peace

1. Any of the following persons shall be punished by imprisonment in the county jail for a period of not more than ninety days, a fine of not more than four hundred dollars ($400), or both such imprisonment and fine:
   a. Any person who unlawfully fights in a public place or challenges another person in a public place to fight.
   b. Any person who maliciously and willfully disturbs another person by loud and unreasonable noise.
2. Any person who uses offensive words in a public place which are inherently likely to provoke an immediate violent reaction.

Nita Criminal Code § 476a—Insufficient Funds Checks

1. Any person who willfully, with intent to defraud, makes or draws or utters or delivers any check for the payment of money, knowing at the time of that making, drawing, uttering, or delivering that the maker has not sufficient funds in, or credit with the bank or depositary for the payment of that check, draft, or order is punishable by imprisonment in a county jail for not more than one year, or in the state prison.

Nita Criminal Code § 487—Theft by False Pretenses

Every person who shall by any false or fraudulent representation or pretense, defraud any other person of money, labor or real or personal property, or who causes or procures others to report falsely of his or her wealth or mercantile character and by thus imposing upon any person, obtains credit and thereby fraudulently gets or obtains possession of money, or property or obtains the labor or service of another, is guilty of theft.

1. Every person who is guilty of the theft of property of a value exceeding four hundred ($400) is guilty of a felony punishable by confinement in prison for one to three years or by confinement in the county jail for up to one year.

2. Theft in other cases is misdemeanor petty theft which is punishable by confinement in the county jail for up to six months, or by a fine of up to one thousand ($1,000), or by both.

Nita Criminal Code § 647(f)—Public Intoxication

Every person who is found in any public place under the influence of intoxicating liquor, any drug, controlled substance, or any combination of any intoxicating liquor, drug, controlled substance, in a condition that he or she is unable to exercise care for his or her own safety or the safety of others, or by reason of his or her being under the influence of intoxicating liquor, any drug, controlled substance, or any combination of any intoxicating liquor, drug, interferes with or obstructs or prevents the free use of any street, sidewalk, or other public way is guilty of a misdemeanor.

Nita Criminal Code § 11350—Possession of a Controlled Substance

1. Every person who possesses any controlled substance which is a narcotic or dangerous drug, unless upon the written prescription of a physician, dentist, podiatrist, or veterinarian licensed to practice in this state, is guilty a felony.

2. A violation of this section shall be punished by imprisonment in the state prison.

Nita Criminal Code § 11357(c)—Possession Marijuana

1. Every person who possesses more than 28.5 grams of marijuana, other than concentrated cannabis, is guilty of a misdemeanor.

2. A violation shall be punished by imprisonment in the county jail for a period of not more than six months or by a fine of not more than five hundred dollars ($500), or by both such fine and imprisonment.

Nita Vehicle Code § 23152(a)—Driving Under the Influence

1. Any person who drives under the influence of any alcoholic beverage or drug is guilty of a misdemeanor.

2. Driving under the influence of alcohol or drugs is a misdemeanor punishable by confinement in the county jail for a period of not more than six months and by a fine of not less than four hundred ($400) nor more than one thousand ($1000).

Nita Vehicle Code § 28051—Unlawful to Alter Indicated Mileage

1. Any person who disconnects, turns back, or resets the odometer of any motor vehicle with intent to alter the number of miles indicated on the odometer gauge is guilty of a misdemeanor.

2. A violation shall be punished by imprisonment in the county jail for a period of not more than six months or by a fine of not more than five hundred dollars ($500), or by both such fine and imprisonment.

Applicable Pennsylvania Criminal Code Section

Pennsylvania Criminal Code § 2504—Involuntary Manslaughter

1. A person commits the crime of involuntary manslaughter when as a direct result of the doing of an unlawful act in a reckless or grossly negligent manner, or the doing of a lawful act in a reckless or grossly negligent manner, he causes the death of another person.
2. Involuntary manslaughter is a felony of the second degree punishable by imprisonment in the state prison for a term of three, four, or five years.

Jury Instructions

State of Nita v. Gene A. Bloodworth

Part I. Preliminary Instructions Given Prior to Evidence

01.01 INTRODUCTION

You have been selected as jurors and have taken an oath to well and truly try this case.

During the progress of the trial, there will be periods of time when the court recesses. During those periods of time, you must not talk to any of the parties, their lawyers, or any of the witnesses.

If any attempt is made by anyone to talk to you concerning the matters here under consideration, you should immediately report that fact to the court.

You should keep an open mind. You should not form or express an opinion during the trial and should reach no conclusion in this case until you have heard all of the evidence, the arguments of counsel, and the final instructions as to the law that will be given to you by the court.

01.02 CONDUCT OF THE TRIAL

First, the attorneys will have an opportunity to make opening statements. These statements are not evidence and should be considered only as a preview of what the attorneys expect the evidence will be.

Following opening statements, witnesses will be called to testify. They will be placed under oath and questioned by the attorneys. Documents and other tangible exhibits may also be received as evidence. If an exhibit is given to you to examine, you should examine it carefully, individually, and without any comment.

It is counsel's right and duty to object when testimony or other evidence is being offered that he or she believes is not admissible.

When the court sustains an objection to a question, you must disregard the question and the answer if one has been given, and draw no inference from the question or answer or speculate as to what the witness would have said if permitted to answer. You must also disregard evidence stricken from the record.

When the court sustains an objection to any evidence, you must disregard that evidence. When the court overrules an objection to any evidence, you must not give that evidence any more weight than if the objection had not been made.

When the evidence is completed, the attorneys will make final statements. These final statements are not evidence but are given to assist you in evaluating the evidence. The attorneys are also permitted to argue in an attempt to persuade you to a particular verdict. You may accept or reject those arguments as you see fit.

Finally, just before you retire to consider your verdict, I will give you further instructions on the law that applies to this case.

Part II. Final Instructions

2.00 RESPECTIVE DUTIES OF JUDGE AND JURY

Ladies and gentlemen of the jury:

You have heard all the evidence and the arguments of the attorneys, and now it is my duty to instruct you on the law. You must arrive at your verdict by unanimous vote applying the law, as you are now instructed, to the facts as you find them to be. The law applicable to this case is stated in these instructions, and it is your duty to follow all of them. You must not single out certain instructions and disregard others.

It is your duty to determine the facts and to determine them only from the evidence in this case. You are to apply the law to the facts and in this way decide the case. You must not be governed or influenced by sympathy or prejudice for or against any party in this case. Your verdict must be based on evidence and not upon speculation, guess, or conjecture.

From time to time, the court has ruled on the admissibility of evidence. You must not concern yourselves with the reasons for these rulings. You should disregard questions and exhibits that were withdrawn or to which objections were sustained. You should also disregard testimony and exhibits that the court has refused or stricken. The evidence that you should consider consists only of the witnesses' testimony and the exhibits the court has received. Any evidence that was received for a limited purpose should not be considered by you for any other purpose. You should consider all the evidence in the light of your own observations and experiences in life.

Neither by these instructions nor by any ruling or remark that I have made do I mean to indicate any opinion as to the facts or as to what your verdict should be.

1.01 CREDIBILITY OF WITNESSES

You are the sole judges of the credibility of the witnesses and of the weight to be given to the testimony of each witness. In determining what credit is to be given any witness, you may take into account the witness's ability and opportunity to observe; the manner and appearance while testifying; any interest, bias, or prejudice the witness may have; the reasonableness of the testimony considered in the light of all the evidence; and any other factors that bear on the believability and weight of the witness's testimony.

1.02 DIRECT AND CIRCUMSTANTIAL EVIDENCE

The law recognizes two kinds of evidence: direct and circumstantial. Direct evidence proves a fact directly; that is, the evidence by itself, if true, established the fact. Circumstantial evidence is the proof of facts or circumstances that give rise to a reasonable inference of other facts; that is, circumstantial evidence proves a fact indirectly in that it follows from other facts or circumstances according to common experience and observations in life. An eyewitness is a common example of direct evidence, while human footprints are circumstantial evidence that a person was present.

The law makes no distinction between direct and circumstantial evidence as to the degree or amount of proof required, and each should be considered according to whatever weight or value it may have. All of the evidence should be considered and evaluated by you in arriving at your verdict.

1.03 "WILLFULLY"—DEFINED

The word "willfully" when applied to the intent with which an act is done or omitted means with a purpose or willingness to commit the act or to make the omission in question. The word "willfully" does not require any intent to violate the law, or to injure another, or to acquire any advantage.

2.01 INFORMATION

The information in this case is the formal method of accusing the defendant of a crime and placing him on trial. It is not any evidence against the defendant and does not create any inference or guilt. The State has the burden of proving beyond a reasonable doubt every essential element of the crimes charged in the information.

2.02 PRESUMPTION OF INNOCENCE

The defendant is presumed to be innocent of the charges against him. This presumption remains with him throughout every stage of the trial and during your deliberations on the verdict. The presumption is not overcome until, from all the evidence in the case, you are convinced beyond a reasonable doubt that the defendant is guilty.

2.03 BURDEN OF PROOF

The State has the burden of proving the guilt of the defendant beyond a reasonable doubt, and this burden remains on the State throughout the case. The defendant is not required to prove his innocence.

2.04 REASONABLE DOUBT

Reasonable doubt means a doubt based upon reason and common sense that arises from a fair and rational consideration of all the evidence or lack of evidence in this case. It is a doubt that is not a vague, speculative, or imaginary doubt, but such a doubt as would cause reasonable persons to hesitate to act in matters of importance to themselves.

2.05 BELIEVABILITY OF A WITNESS—CONVICTION OF A CRIMINAL OFFENSE

The fact that a witness has been convicted of a criminal offense, if such be a fact, may be considered by you only for the purpose of determining the believability of that witness. The fact of such a conviction does not necessarily destroy or impair a witness's believability. It is one of the circumstances that you may take into consideration in weighing the testimony of such a witness.

2.06 MOTIVE

Motive is not an element of the crimes charged and need not be shown. However, you may consider motive or lack of motive as a circumstance in this case. Presence of motive may tend to establish guilt. Absence of motive may tend to establish innocence. You will therefore give its presence or absence, as the case may be, the weight to which you find it to be entitled.

2.07 DEFENDANT NOT TESTIFYING—NO INFERENCE OF GUILT MAY BE DRAWN

A defendant in a criminal trial has a constitutional right not to be compelled to testify. You must not draw any inference from the fact that a defendant does not testify. Further, you must neither discuss this matter nor permit it to enter into your deliberations in any way.

2.08 EXPERT TESTIMONY

A person is qualified to testify as an expert if they have special knowledge, skill, experience, training, or education sufficient to qualify them as an expert on the subject to which the testimony relates.

You are not bound to accept an expert opinion as conclusive, but should give to it the weight to which you find it to be entitled. You may disregard any such opinion if you find it to be unreasonable.

3.00 CHARGES

The State of Nita has charged the defendant, Gene Bloodworth, with the crime of first degree murder, which includes the crimes of second degree murder, manslaughter, and criminally negligent homicide. If you are not satisfied beyond a reasonable doubt that the defendant is guilty of the crime charged, you may nevertheless convict the defendant of any lesser crime, if you are convinced beyond a reasonable doubt that the defendant is guilty of such lesser crime. The defendant has pled not guilty.

3.01 FIRST DEGREE MURDER

Under the Criminal Code of the State of Nita, a person commits the crime of first degree murder if, after deliberation and with the intent to cause the death of a person other than himself, he or she causes the death of another person.

A person acts intentionally with respect to a result or to conduct described by a statute defining a crime when his or her conscious objective is to cause such result or to engage in such conduct.

Deliberation means that a decision to commit the act has been made after the exercise of reflection and judgment concerning the act.

To sustain the charge of first degree murder the State must prove:

1) That the defendant performed the acts which caused the death of Kenneth Fletcher; and

2) That the defendant acted after deliberation and with the intent to cause the death of Kenneth Fletcher.

If you find from your consideration of all the evidence that each of these propositions has been proved beyond a reasonable doubt, then you should find the defendant guilty of first degree murder.

If, on the other hand, you find from your consideration of all the evidence that any of these propositions has not been proved beyond a reasonable doubt, then you should find the defendant not guilty of first degree murder.

3.02 SECOND DEGREE MURDER

Under the Criminal Code of the State of Nita, a person commits the crime of second degree murder if:

1) He or she intentionally, but not after deliberation, causes the death of a person; or

2) With intent to cause serious injury to a person other than himself or herself, he or she causes the death of that person or of another person.

A person acts intentionally with respect to a result or to conduct described by a statute defining a crime when his or her conscious objective is to cause such result or to engage in such conduct.

To sustain the charge of second degree murder, the State must prove the following propositions:

1) That the defendant performed the acts which caused the death of Kenneth Fletcher; and

2) That the defendant intended to kill or cause serious bodily injury to Kenneth Fletcher.

If you find from your consideration of all the evidence that each of these propositions has been proven beyond a reasonable doubt, then you should find the defendant guilty of second degree murder.

If, on the other hand, you find from your consideration of all the evidence that any of these propositions has not been proved beyond a reasonable doubt, then you should find the defendant not guilty of second degree murder.

3.03 VOLUNTARY MANSLAUGHTER

Under the Criminal Code of the State of Nita, a person commits the crime of voluntary manslaughter if:

1) He or she intentionally, but not after deliberation, causes the death of a person under circumstances where the act causing the death was performed upon a sudden heat of passion caused by a serious and highly provoking act of the intended victim, affecting the person killing sufficiently to excite an irresistible passion in a reasonable person. However, if between the provocation and the killing there is an interval sufficient for the voice of reason and humanity to be heard, the killing is murder.

To sustain the charge of voluntary manslaughter, the State must prove that the defendant intentionally caused the death of Kenneth Fletcher under circumstances where the act causing death was performed upon a sudden heat of passion caused by a serious and highly provoking act of the intended victim, Kenneth Fletcher.

If you find from your consideration of all the evidence that this proposition has been proved beyond a reasonable doubt, then you should find the defendant guilty of voluntary manslaughter.

If, on the other hand, you find from your consideration of all the evidence that this proposition has not been proved beyond a reasonable doubt, then you should find the defendant not guilty of voluntary manslaughter.

3.04 CRIMINALLY NEGLIGENT HOMICIDE

Under the Criminal Code of the State of Nita, a person commits the crime of criminally negligent homicide if:

1) By conduct amounting to criminal negligence he or she causes the death of a person; or

2) He or she intentionally causes the death of a person, but believes in good faith that circumstances exist which would justify his or her conduct, but that belief that such circumstances exist is unreasonable.

Conduct means an act or omission and its accompanying state of mind, or a series of acts or omissions.

A person acts with criminal negligence when, through a gross deviation from the standard of care that a reasonable person would exercise, he or she fails to perceive a substantial and unjustifiable risk that a result will occur or that a circumstance exists.

To sustain the charge of criminally negligent homicide the State must provide the following propositions:

1) That the defendant performed the acts which caused the death of Kenneth Fletcher, and

2) That the defendant acted with criminal negligence, or he acted intentionally, but believed in good faith that circumstances existed which would have justified the killing of Kenneth Fletcher, and his belief that such circumstances existed was unreasonable.

If you find from your consideration of all the evidence that each of these propositions has been proved beyond a reasonable doubt, then you should find the defendant guilty of criminally negligent homicide.

If, on the other hand, you find from your consideration of all the evidence that either of these propositions has not been proved beyond a reasonable doubt, then you should find the defendant not guilty of criminally negligent homicide.

3.10 SELF-DEFENSE

The killing of another person in self-defense is justifiable and not unlawful when the person who does the killing actually and reasonably believes:

1) That there is imminent danger that the other person will either kill him or cause him great bodily harm; and

2) That it was necessary under the circumstances for him to use in self-defense such force or means as might cause the death of the other person, for the purpose of avoiding death or great bodily injury to himself.

A bare fear of death or great bodily injury is not sufficient to justify a homicide. To justify taking the life of another in self-defense, the circumstances must be such as to excite the fears of a reasonable person placed in a similar position, and the party killing must act under the influence of such fears alone. The danger must be apparent, present, immediate and instantly dealt with, or so must appear at the time to the slayer as a reasonable person, and the killing must be done under a well-founded belief that it is necessary to save one's self from death or great bodily harm.

The State has the burden to prove that the killing was not in lawful self-defense. If you have a reasonable doubt that such was unlawful, then you must find the defendant not guilty.

4.01 JURY MUST NOT CONSIDER PENALTY

In your deliberations do not discuss or consider the subject of penalty or punishment. That subject must not in any way affect your verdict.

4.02 CONCLUDING INSTRUCTION

You shall now retire and select one of your number to act as presiding juror. He or she will preside over your deliberations. In order to reach a verdict, all jurors must agree to the decision. As soon as all of you have agreed upon a verdict, so that each may state truthfully that the verdict expresses his or her vote, have it dated and signed by your presiding juror and return with it to the courtroom.

IN THE DISTRICT COURT
OF THE STATE OF NITA
COUNTY OF DARROW

THE STATE OF NITA	)	
	)	Case No. CR 2201-05
v.	)	
	)	
GENE A. BLOODWORTH,	)	JURY VERDICT
Defendant.	)	
	)	

We, the jury, return the following verdict, and each of us concurs in this verdict:

[Choose the appropriate verdict]

I. NOT GUILTY

We, the jury, find the defendant, Gene A. Bloodworth, NOT GUILTY.

_____
Presiding Juror

II. GUILTY

We, the jury, find the defendant, Gene A. Bloodworth, GUILTY of the crime of:

Murder in the first degree   _____

Murder in the second degree   _____

Voluntary manslaughter   _____

Criminally negligent homicide   _____

_____
Presiding Juror